A BUNCH OF KEYS
Selected Poems by
Mutsuo Takahashi

A BUNCH OF KEYS

Selected Poems by
MUTSUO TAKAHASHI

Translated by
Hiroaki Sato

With an Introduction by
Robert Peters

THE CROSSING PRESS
Trumansburg, New York 14886

Books by Hiroaki Sato

History, criticism, etc.:
One Hundred Frogs: From Renga to Haiku to English
Translations:
Poems of Princess Shikishi
Ten Japanese Poets
Spring & Asura: Poems of Kenji Miyazawa
Mutsuo Takahashi: Poems of a Penisist
Lilac Garden: Poems of Minoru Yoshioka
Howling at the Moon: Poems of Hagiwara Sakutaro
See You Soon: Poems of Taeko Tomioka
Chieko and Other Poems of Takamura Kotaro
with Burton Watson:
From the Country of Eight Islands

Cover design and section dividers by David Ruether
Cover photo by Eikoh Hosoe
Frontispiece photo by Taiji Arita
Book design by Allison Platt
Typesetting by M.J. Waters

Library of Congress Cataloging in Publication Data

Takahashi, Mutsuo, 1937-
    A bunch of keys.

    Translation of: Kagitaba.
    Includes bibliographies.
    1. Homosexuality, Male--Poetry. I. Sato, Hiroaki,
1942-   . II. Title.
PL862.A4212K313 1984   895.6'15   84-16964
ISBN 0-89594-145-7 (hard)
ISBN 0-89594-144-9 (pbk.)

Introduction

The appearance of Mitsuo Takahashi's Selected Poems: *A Bunch of Keys* should further enhance the reputation he earned with his *Poems of a Penisist,* published in 1975 by the Chicago Review Press. In their sexual frankness, a mix of funk and idealism, *Penisist* seemed in advance of its time, as a fresh, vibrant celebration of homosexual love. Only Ginsberg's *Howl* surpassed Takahashi's poem in its wild power. And certainly Takahashi owes much to Ginsberg. Both, as celebrative writers of scope (Ginsberg intent on excoriating American culture in the 50s; Takahashi, more private, luxuriating in the worlds of male sex as symbolic settings for the penisist's drive to fill a modern Existentialist void) owed much to Whitman and his long free verse lines sprawled over the pages like husky arms waiting to grope you, his catalogues, his unabashed exuberance for the body as a reflection of the spirit. Lorca too comes to mind. Lorca was, of course, influenced by Whitman—his "Ode to Walt Whitman" is a modern classic of homosexual pain and joy, written in Whitman's mode.

Takahashi's book, after the initial piece about a poet's suicide, opens calmly enough—these early poems nibble our consciousness via traditional images: swirling stars, blowing wind, lone cypress trees, storms in the heart, vague yearnings, boys with gentle and calm eyes—all tame stuff. Then, with "At A Throat" something happens—motifs of pursuit, coarse sexual assault, and razor-sharp lust appear. Fury and sweat are motifs now seldom absent from this volume.

No poet I know relishes sex as much as Takahashi. The incredible "Ode" which runs for some 40 pages, is an incredible panegyric to the glorious stink of male sex. For this, the poem earns its place on the shelf alongside the Boyd MacDonald anthologies. A portion of "Ode" is devoted to *Groin Odor:* smells of burnt metal, fire, spices, suffocating flowers, saddle on which a naked man rides, spilled blood, a woodcutter's stout thighs devoured by wild dogs, forest smells (rotting leaves, earthworms, etc.), saliva on a savage's lips, outlaw smells, sea-smells, clam smells. The *Prick* itself is a "sleeping baby rabbit," or a dove at rest, or any number of glorious creatures animate and inanimate. Fucking itself is seen as a wielding of knives and spears:

A spear pierces a pliant youth, its spearhead upright
The red hot blade, the cutting edge of a sword,
    the blade of a hatchet, the blade of a kitchen knife...

The Turkish bath, the tea room, and cock-cheese all come in for
cataloguing and praise. One wonderfully erotic moment is this, when
the penisist grabs the shaft of another man:

There, I caught you
Lovely male rabbit
held down in my hands, you bounce
With vigor, like a spring
Like the tip of a fountain pressed under the hand
    of a naughty boy...

The entire ode proceeds towards the men's room, and the ubiquitous
glory hole. Fantasies galore: Takahashi's head-givers are
hunks—soldiers, line-men, police-men, sailors—all beautiful, all
young, all like outlaw figures from Genet's novels, each with his own
amoralities. In a parody of Rodin's statue "The Thinker," Takahashi's
cocksucker sits on his haunches, on the porcelain john, "thinking,"
waiting for the next shaft to come ramming through (the hole has
been fixed up with a sponge and encircled by a drawing of a vagina).
Takahashi's *thinker* has his metaphysics: he is the "pray-er" who
"waits eagerly for the visitation of the penis, the supernatural, through
the holy hole, i.e., for the visitation of the heavenly to the earthly."
Here Takahashi seems to be glossing what he learned from his friend
Yukio Mishima—the Void *is* the glory-hole, and the human mouth,
better than the anus or the vagina is the archetypal void that the
driven cocksucker craves to fill, as an antidote to his "loneliness."

Next in interest are 24 self-portraits—the poet as a traveler, a
troubador, as king of the wood, as an ancient goddess, as an ancient
Queen, as Telemachus, as Narcissus, as a motor-bike rider, as at-
tendant of "the last fire." These are much more tightly written than the
Ode, and are just as passionate and as humorous (don't overlook the
considerable humor in Takahashi). Takahashi shifts continually
before our eyes. I like him best in these various guises, when he has
gotten himself up from that Rodinesque position on the john and
regales us with his dancing shifts of persona and costume.

Robert Peters
Huntington Beach, California

Translator's Note and Acknowledgment

This is the second selection of Mutsuo Takahashi's poems I've translated. The first, *Poems of a Penisist,* was published in 1975 by Chicago Review Press. One poem has been carried over from that selection: *Ode,* which Takahashi has revised. Some of the other translations in this book first appeared in *From the Country of Eight Islands* and *Gay Shunshine.*

I decided to use no footnotes; Takahashi is frequently allusive, but his allusion seldom obfuscates. The footnotes to "*Ode:* Afterword" are Takahashi's own.

I thank Takahashi for answering questions about his poems and assembling photographs for illustration; Robert Fagan, Nancy Rossiter, and Burton Watson for helping me translate these poems; Rand Castile for reading the manuscript carefully; and John Gill for spending a whole evening with me to make this book a reality. I dedicate these translations to Robert Fagan.

Hiroaki Sato
Spring 1984

Table of Contents

from **A Bunch of Keys**

from

AT A PLACE
CALLED WANDERING

(1958-1961; published 1979)

Poet's Love

The earth is burning.
The stone city explodes like an ammunition dump.
In the flames the poet finally puts a gun to his forehead.
Under his disheveled hair, from the cracked flesh a golden cranium peers
and illuminates bodies of flesh, dead or on the brink of death.
The holy men under the oak tree are praying in a halo of suffering.
The widow goes, crying, crying, holding the hand of her barefoot child.
Hagar, Hagar, why are you crying?
Will the widow be able to meet a powerful chest under a hemp palm?
Will the boy be able to hold, in the blue night, the thighs in rough soldier pants
and feel a big hand in his hair?
In the distance the city is still thundering.

Small Poem

A dirty tub in which feet have been washed

Hands that tear bread for the poor

On the wooden table a cup with water

Light

Outside the window a stone-pear tree

Or   a peach tree with fruit as hard as stones

On the road   in the darkness that has already descended

Guest and master holding each other

Night

Tell me about your night.
The stars are swirling.
The earth is listening.
Putting up with the wind blowing intently,

a single cypress, standing there,
is like a pale palm of a hand.
Hair that crawls up—but
that palm, what is that palm waiting for?

Yet tell me also about those who cannot sleep,
your swirling night above their heads.
He pushes his window open and, letting the night blow on his flaming
      head,

is putting up with the terrible storm that rushes through his heart.
Those lamps of houses that are so bright they make one feel sad—
what do they look like in his eyes?

Yearnings

Well then, you begin with vague yearnings.
Distant cypress—
begin with the highway where heat haze is rising,
the bright sun of May shining on it.

Begin with travelers hurrying
here and there, staring at their shadows, sun on their backs.
Begin with an inn beyond the deeply fragrant wood,
waiting for the travelers, its sign swaying.

The window merely thundering, reflecting the blue sky—
soon a storm will come and make it flutter.
Then, for the first time you may push the wall,

go out under the maddening sky
which sorrows, snuggling together, support,
and sing your own song.

To a Boy

Boy,
you are a hidden watering place under the trees
where, as the day darkens, gentle beasts with calm eyes
appear one after another.

Even if the sun drops flaming at the end of the fields where grass stirs
    greenly
and a wind pregnant with coolness and night-dew agitates your leafy
    bush,
it is only a premonition.

The tree of solitude that soars with ferocity,
crowned with a swirling night,
still continues to sleep in your dark place.

At a Throat

Fury—iron swung down,
then, black fleeing in many blue nights.
For a while through the trees your face, now a pulpy mess, chased
    me,
closed eyelashes trembling as if they wanted to say something.
But I no longer envy your gentle throat.
What has come between you and me:
an act, a crime—and, time.
                                        Hot morning, throat gurgling,
I drink water. Sweat turns into beads, blankets my forehead, and
    trembles.
Reflected in the sweat beads, a breeze from a tamarisk is trembling.
I take a plow in my arms of solitude and, in the deep noon, become a
    man.
That pitiful fellow—I divide the coarse soil into two strands of soil
and, back turned to the noon where silence resounds, and plowing,
walk step by step toward the evening with lightning flaring in the
    clouds.
—In the barn's cold darkness gleams a razor-sharp sickle.

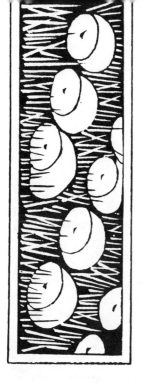

from

YOU DIRTY ONES,
DO DIRTIER THINGS!

(1961-1966; published 1966)

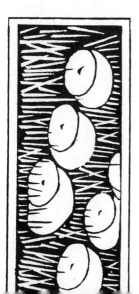

The Lust of the Eyes, or the Tribe of Eagles

For all that *is* in the world, the lust of the flesh, and the lust of the eyes, and the pride of life, is not of the Father, but is of the world. And the world passeth away, and the lust thereof. . . .

The First Epistle General of John 2:16-17

1. Seer's Misfortune

For me to see is salt.
For my seeing there is no cure.
A tree standing, a flock of thrushes dropping, at the distant end of my
    vision,
become painful foreign objects, stab the flesh of my eyes.

By the incessant thirst for seeing
my eyes have been scraped inwardly into conic shapes.
For me to see is relentless gimlet-twisting.
There is no water, no shadow, for consolation.

2. Peerer

The peerer's eyeballs are bone-dry;
sucked to the spindle-shaped keyhole
they are connected to the blind holes of the sockets
with many bloodshot strands of flesh.

The jealousy-mixed, pulsating desire
to see other people's happiness
makes the sockets smart with thirst and rubs with envy
the eyeballs at the end of the strands, fiercely hurting them.

In the elastic skinbag, below the pointed bones,
his blatant stomach goes up and down;
in it, terribly bitter, but thin,
something watery is making a gurgling noise.

3. Valery's Night

There's something called a night of storm.
Inside the room with the iron blinds solemnly lowered
the youth, furrowing his brow, is staring at the fire
built like a stack of arms on the iron support in the fireplace.
Or reading a book in his lap.
The pliant branches of trees he can't see
touch the outside of the double door.
—There's that noise.

Abruptly, truly of a sudden,
inside the tree of vigorous flames
one clean decision rises to its feet.
Or from between the precise lines of the opened book
one thought begins to shine.
Within the youth, music fiercely boils.
Around him all noises cease
and in a vacuum of all meanings, he is the epicenter.

The next morning, taking his overcoat from the hook at the door
he suddenly sets out on an aimless journey
or immerses himself in endless adventure in the wood of geometry.
For her son who has become a stranger overnight
his mother, timidly, worriedly,
pours tea.

4. Summons

A pomegranate. A tamarisk by the water.
Bundles of wheat dried and thrashed. Honeybees' peaceful murmurs.
Doves, and tame camels.
The stone entrance to the deserted yard of a synagogue.
In its shadow, standing barefoot, head down,
the boy was absorbed in reading the book of law.
It was him you suddenly took.

It was by force, peremptory,
exactly in the manner
of assaulting a girl full of shame.
I was wrestled down, abused,
and my young mouth
was blindly pushed into
by an invisible powerful hand.

When I came to, I'd been discarded.
The doves had flown away, and not a single one was left.
The leaves of the trees had blown off, the sky muddy.
The gentle face of the landscape that surrounded me
now felt coarse, sand collecting,
and looked at me as though in a foul mood.
I went out of my father's house.

I went out into the wasteland.
I sipped dew, chewed on pigpeas.
Still you did not relax your pursuit
but often assaulted me.
My mouth was ordered to say specific things.
My mouth spewed curse words
terrifying to my own ear.

14

Kings came, threatened me,
and discarded me in a mudhole in their yard.
Into that smelly hole, too, you came.
Toward me sinking in the muddy bottom
you threw not bread
but the vinegar and sponge of fierce damnation
that on the contrary led to hunger and thirst.

5. Colon on Board a Ship

St. Cristobal Colon.
On the fist of his left hand
a brilliantly colored talking bird.
In his right hand, weighty binoculars.

With his eyes he can see
the sacred new continent receding,
even that invisible dark worm
that devours God's naive children.

His right leg is discoverer's gold.
But his left leg is a rotting column
entwined with syphilitic tropical-flower ropes.

On his earth-hued forehead, already death's profuse sweat.
Enduring the weight of the radial halo
his sturdy shoulders tilt.

6. Dark Orpheus

His right eye is a sun,
his left eye a malicious moon.
That half of his body with the eye of the sun is full of flesh and glitters,
but that side with the moon is feeble and crooked, moist as an amphibian.

At the top of a rock mountain, innumerable leaves swimming in the light.
The sky's thunderous silence, the avalanching blue.
His bright half flaps
toward things clean, things supreme,

but sinking in the darkness, his other half leans
toward maggots, toward the steep slope to the dark country.
Rather, leaning, he himself
is a voiceless dark country.

7. An Image of Dante Alighieri

To look at Paradise is terrifying,
to look at what is holiest, which night and day
angels who are called light, innumerable as summer flies,
protect, incessantly buzzing, quivering their six wings that radiate glittery crystals.

On the flesh behind your eyes layers of scabs form,
and the smelly juice that oozes out of the gaps of your lowered
eyelashes congeals into wax.
You become a repulsive blind man and must wander,
pointed at, whispered about, from one unknown country to another.

You, as I know you, are like that.

8. Jacob Bohme's Tin Bowl

A shoe-tree. A leather knife. A half-made shoe.
A sturdy wooden box containing nails. A hammer. A plate of water.
    Fire.
And scattered all about, strips of leather—
that is, devotion and sacrifice in many forms for the glory called
    shoes.

Radiation of cracks—the painful light that shines in the clouded high
    window where a spider lurks
has caught the humblest thing among the humble things:
a shabby tin bowl that offers a dull reflection as a hesitant gift in
    return,
a poor bowl assigned to the simple task of boiling.

On the surface of the modest metal, the light uttered a voice
which sounded hurt and at the same time joyful.
This way, the noble lightbeam and the base metal caressed each
    other
and, like dark lovers, sobbed funereally.

9. Jeanne d'Arc Being Tried

In the middle of shaggy hair, idiotic,
twitching pale like a frog, a small face full of freckles.
Her eyes, muddy, jaundiced, dull as winter sunlight—
what on earth do you say they saw?

Outside this empty well, strewn with snotty tissue,
orange peels, an old comb stuck with hair, and filth,
winter clouds sharply split, a rope ladder lowered—
what kind of god do you say came down?

Dumb people who, saliva at the edges of their mouths, swear and spit
     phlegm—
this dog-like girl, whose soul the terror and the cold deprived,
cannot even feel that.

The phrase, "de profundis," does not exist here.
What is here is only the most miserable flesh,
frightened, freezing, as it was discarded even by heaven.

10. To John in The Revelation

All the terrifying incidents
are not in time,
not in visible space,
but behind your feverish eyelids,
in the eyes that continue to bulge grotesquely.

Packing billions of screams
in the darkness of the irises the size of a needle-hole
your eyes are on the brink of blowing up.
Your entire existence, in unison,
gathers in the pulsating eyeballs.

LEGEND OF A GIANT

(1967; published 1978)

Legend of a Giant

To Ernesto Che Guevara

Baje Grande's ravaged horizon. Above it, a spherical sky.
Your head is like a football; jumping up and staying there,
it has become a new heavenly body that keeps turning a cursed
perpetual motion.
Your two diamonds, the two eyeballs, have become two invisible
stars of the first magnitude
of an invisible constellation on the inner wall of noon's celestial
sphere.
Your heart, sucked in by a terrible hole on the other side of the earth,
has become a pump of fury in the ground that blows up every single
volcano.
Your blood that keeps breaking out of blood vessels and overflowing
has become a viscous heavy sea.
The brilliantly colored intestines, wet like fish, have become lands on
a map afloat in the sea.
Your bones and skin have become the sky's keel and the fluttering
tent put up across it.
Your hair has become stands of wild sugar cane that bury the earth.
Your breath has become the hot winds contained in the sky above the
sugar cane.
Your saliva has become the dark water circulating in the network of
labyrinths at the bottom of the dry ground.
Your semen has become crystals of salt hidden in the rock floors of
steep mountains.
All plants hold the crystals with the tips of their secretive roots,
all animals lick the crystals with their gentle tongues.

Torn apart, how large you have become!

* * *

Further, you do not remain that size.
Because you continue to bulge, single-mindedly continue to bulge,
because memories of your flesh were, in particular, roses and lilies,
the miserable earth and the layers of celestial spheres that pile upon it
fill with innumerable lilies and roses that continue to bulge:

lilies of the forehead, lilies of the breast, lilies of the back, lilies of the
   thighs,
roses of the eyes, roses of the lips, roses of the heart, roses of the
   navel—
below the celestial spheres of burning roses, above the earth covered
   with frozen lilies
(or else, below the sky of ice-bound lilies, above the earth of flaming
   roses)
a single, abandoned balcony
where, beating my breast, scattering ashes of sorrow over my head,
or becoming the single point of a gimlet being sucked into the sky of
   roses,
I, a wailing woman, imitate that classical form of grief.
You, who have become too large, are no longer mine.
I will collect the materials of my inner grief and, once again, re-create
   you, from the beginning point, a single cell.

   * * *

The ants of time visibly devour the real you.
By the reverse method I re-create you from the beginning.
Even so, what were you?
(Bearded revolutionary? Phantom guerrilla leader?)
In order to mold you newly and make you rise to your feet,
what kind of fire, soil, and water do I have to knead
in my hot oven of pining for you, in what proportions, by which
   technique?
(You're a strategist smelling of soil, mountain water, salted pork, and
   outdoor fires?)
Which roses in my blood, which lilies in my semen,
shall I gather to make your exquisite body?
(Your straightforwardness and modesty! Boundless generosity and
   depth of hatred!)
Truly, you're a tower of lilies with lilies piled, lilies stacked.
The coldness of lilies, warmth of lilies, lasciviousness of lilies,
   fastidiousness of lilies—
even if what is transported inside them is the roses of life,
on what foundation shall I make
your rare muscles, rare gentleness, rare scrotum?
What kind of alchemist shall I become to resuscitate you?

24

No, this wasn't it. Let's begin once again.

* * *

Shall I become a hunchbacked smith for you
to hammer out your indestructible iron heart?
Shall I become a blind grape crusher for you
to ferment a bubbling wine that courses through your body?
Shall I become a crippled tanner for you
to line the two tough bellows in your chest?
Shall I become a deaf boiler tender for you
to blow hot breaths into your bellows?
Shall I become a dumb baker for you
to mold your tender brain and firm scrotum?
Shall I become a harelipped beekeeper for you
to refine your sweet, highly viscid brains and semen?
Shall I become a gouty tailor for you
to sew a skin to contain your gentleness and sturdiness?
Shall I become a lead-poisoned precious metal craftsman for you
to forge your soul of pure gold that governs the entire you?

No, this won't do, this wasn't it, either.

* * *

The two pure materials from which the entire you derives,
your scrotum and your thought—I separate them on the two pans of a
    balance.
Your scrotum is a pigskin bag extended with water, droplets
    sprouting on its surface.
Your thought is the steamy air around the bag.
Your scrotum is a productive tropical tree spreading its branches.
Your thought is its sweet, heavy fruit.
Your scrotum is a seething midday bullring.
Your thought is the shouts that overflow into the sky above the bull-
    ring.
Your scrotum is a magic rope of garlic hanging at the door.
Your thought is its powerful smell that pervades the air.
Your scrotum is a gold nugget just dug out.
Your thought is the dazzle around that nugget.

Scrotum and thought—let's reverse the pans of the balance—thought
    and scrotum.

Your thought: the clarity of fierce rapids.
Your scrotum: the murkiness of the lake that gives birth to the fierce
    rapids.
Your thought: the swiftness of a hawk aiming at its prey.
Your scrotum: the sturdy arm letting the hawk rest.
Your thought: the glitter of spilling salt.
Your scrotum: the tilted pot of salt.
Your thought: the far-offness of ships.
Your scrotum: the horizon that sends out the fleet.
Your thought: the chaos of a nebula.
Your scrotum: the blue sky that allows the nebula to exist—

      * * *

These, the words that trace you.
The painful relics of you, a splendid structure.
Words are empty. I'll turn around to the backside of the relics.
Then, behold, in the leaden daybreak sky I have not known,
your thought, brazenly taking the form of the scrotum,
hangs with gentle weightiness and, enveloped by admiring vultures,
grows vague in many layers as it sways, continues to sway.
Before I know it, around it, pubic hair of clouds that press in from the
    horizon in the four directions—
fierce blood vessels of lightning cleave over the thighs of the at-
    mosphere.
I will go out, like that ancient female deity,
as an eternal wanderer, into the world,
into the wasteland of the hearts of those people I love, who look ex-
    actly like wild dogs feasting on carrion.
I will go to look for and collect you, torn apart and scattered,
in particular, your penis, bloody, solitary in the rubble.

ODE

*(1966-1970; first published 1971;
published in revised form 1980)*

In the name of
man, member,
and the holy fluid,
AMEN

Ode

There is a sunset
The world's most tragic
Therefore the most beautiful sunset
The hypersensitive skin of "time" that shifts every sec-
ond
The world's rosy urticaria—against it
Towering dark, facing this way, a MAN

MAN Both his pained face, slightly looking down, on a sturdy
neck
Of many muscles, of gnarled twisted sinews
And the bulges of flesh on his chest
Draped with curled hairs, each hard as wire
Are sealed in shadow's domain, indistinct
But where his powerful loins—which in a distant dazzl-
ing century
Of gold spurted Adam's healthy sons—
Join the monolithic flesh-filled crotch
The sacred center brimming with fertile power lies in
the light
There in the hair, the downy grass licked, washed,
cared for
Strand by strand by the gentle tongue of light
Rests dormant the beautiful flesh
Look closely: from its root to its festering wine-colored
tip
It is plastered with a sheet of horrible ants of pleasure
Some coming in and out of the holes they bored
The man's expression that looked as if it did not move
Is slowly moving, invisible to the eye
Tenses into the form of wrath the two vines of blood
vessels

That entwine his thick neck—
Only, the waves of pain that swell up from his dim
 underbelly
Move like the breathing earth, rising and falling, so
 slow
One cannot see it clearly
—Now, his ponderous head imperceptively tilts
And the wrinkles of pain that have caught his face like
 a net
Fleetingly mimic a delightfully laughing childlike face
This towering man does not have an arm, chopped at
 the shoulder
The lost arm, gaining the weight of gold, flows away
Horizontally in the river against a distant sunset, a
 salmon-colored sky
To this drifting sacred relic cling innumerable red ants
No, abominable women criers, hair covered with ash
The "pheasant weepers"
The obscene wailings of these women strike heaven
As the arm of gold moves little by little, to the west, to
 the west
Indifferent to the gloomy distant landscape—but
This man, blissfully suffering, sinks little by little
Sinks, and soon he will become invisible
Will leave only an earth-like vomit, like afterbirth
An ending of a great drama that was
Shall we call this a downfall?

Quo Vadis?
Where?
Where on earth are you going?
Please do not go
Please stay
For that I would kneel, I would kiss
The skin of your soles, turned moist, white, flaccid in
    the shoes
Smelly from the greasy socks, your feet

TOE JAM Your toes, rolling upward, nails storing dark-blue dirt
Let me give them passionate kisses repeatedly
The four spaces between the toes, four small darkness-
    es infested with fungi
Backs of the arrogant toes, the arches clammy with
    sweat
The knotty ankles, the calves, the hams
Do accept
The wet admiration of my tongue and lips that climb
    leisurely
Above these, there are two splendid pillars
Entasis columns, cruel cracks running over them
The part further up, lost in a cloud of overwhelming
    fragrance, is invisible

GROIN A perfumed oil factory, the darkness of its storehouse,
ODOR   and in the deeper darkness
Inside its irregular, dusty pots, heavy perfumed oils un-
    dulate separately
In a vat, pomade kneaded with bamboo spatulas
    shines green
The perfumed oil of nard rubbed on the thighs, down
    to the shins
Of a bullfighter in a tight corset
The young smell of olive oil which the youths
Of the gymnasiums of ancient Greece
Rub on one another's naked skin, some standing, some
    bending
The smells of the balm, frankincense, myrrh, cin-
    namon of the mummies
That suspend the flowery death of young Egyptian
    nobles

The smells of the oil rubbed on a rifle, of an armory, of
    gasoline
The smell of heavy oil spreading rainbow-colored on
    the sea, over a sunken ship
Smell of iron, smell of iron rust, smell of solder
Smell of metal burnt off by a blowtorch
Smell of the dark of a smith's shop
Smell of the cord short-circuited late on a cold night
Smell of the lightning that struck, smell of a fire, smell
    of flint, smell of an ignitor
A power box, gunsmoke, cartridges, their smells
A coffee grinder, pepper grinder, muller, their smells
Smells of spices cramming the spice shelves
Of a spacious kitchen that the cooks guard
Clouds of spices, clouds of flowers
The suffocating smells of flowers
Grown in a green house covered with a glass-paned
    ceiling
Milk vetch carpeting the field, a carpet of rape flowers
The alfalfa crushed by a young steed as it trots past,
    led by its trainer
Wood-sorrels, hare's-ears, dayflowers in the shadow,
    wild grasses, their smells
The azure coast, the perfume town of Grasse
Jasmine, violet, that grow in the fields under fierce sun
Mimosa, genista, that spew golden fire
Heliotrope, lilac, magnolia, their smells
The smell of lavender that is particularly manly
Smell of a strong perfume soaked into Grasse leather
Tanned hides hanging from a tanner's ceiling
Piles of a shoemaker's leather scraps, the strop the
    barber sharpens his razors on, their smells
The smell of the saddle, still raw, painful to the naked
    thighs
Smell of the young horse's wound covered irritably by
    blue flies
Smell of spilled blood, smell of blood plasma
Smell of a woodcutter's stout thighs a pack of wild
    dogs devours
Smell of the forest, smell of fallen leaves, rotting leaves

Beneath the rotting leaves, earthworms, sow bugs,
  centipedes, their smells
Smells of nuts, the acorns, honey locusts, hazels
The sunny smell of a pasania nut as it pops
Smell of bones washed brownish white by rains and
  winds
Smell of a tile made of the bone of a solitary desert
  animal
Smell of a copper thrown on a sheepskin spread on the
  sand
Smell of the saliva foaming around savage men's lips
Smell of the palm smelly with sweat
Smell of vagrancy, smell of an outlaw
The leather belts men wear around their waists to carry
  swords
The machete drawn with a flourish, its cool blue smell
Smell of the sea, smell of coppers on a littoral
Smell of navigation, sails tattered in wind and rain
Worm-eaten decks, hawsers that squeak, their smells
Smell of brine, separate routes, separate ports, their
  smells
Here now is London, a basement pub that smells of
  men
Male Britons crack traditional solemn jokes
And never smiling themselves
Puff Havana cigars clenched in their white teeth, that
  smell of tobacco
The men, impeccable dandies in every way
But totally indifferent to the nicotine that burns their
  nails, that smell
For the pleasure of a long winter hibernation, out of
  oblivion and dust
They take out their pipes made of rose roots from cold
  wastelands
Clean and polish them, their smell
Smell of roses, smell of a rose perfume, the cut tobac-
  co moist with perfume
Smell of soap, smell of a bathroom
Eau de cologne, smell of lotions that smell of men
The Roko oil, the brilliantine fragrant on a young man's

sideburns in a risque print
Smell of freshly washed indigo
Smell of the sooty fireplace in an old mansion, smell of
the fire in bygone days
Smell of the stove
Smell of the coal that bare chilblained hands pick and
add
Smell of powdered coal, smell of the fire made in a
powdered coal dump on a cold morning
Smell of the yawn of a young bum warming himself by
the fire
Smell of hunger
Smell of the station where trains are rushed in and out
Smell of the grime in the waiting room criss-crossed
with steam pipes
Smell of a cheap hotel, smell of the room for men
Smells of a prison, dormitory, army, the smell of war
Coarse khaki overcoats, military uniforms, boots,
knapsacks, their smells
Smell of the blanket one pulls up with both hands to
one's mouth
Smell of an army on the move, smell of a retreat, smell
of reticence
Smell of a march, rain never ceasing
Rubber boots, the insides of sweaty rubber coats, their
smells
Smells of puddles, smell of marshes
The ditch outside a public bathhouse at one a.m., the
steam rising from the waste water, that smell
Smell of raw garbage rotting inexorably in a polyethy-
lene bucket
Smell of fermented rice, smell of yeast
Inside the steamer, the smell of the warm leaven
Smell of the country sink outlet where water-hemlocks
flourish
Smell of the flesh of a clam as it opens in tepid water in
the sun
The finger, rotten purple, its joint bound with tough
thread
Smell of the finger that crushed an insect, smell of the

firefly's crushed tail
Elderberry bush growing in delicate shadows, smell of
  summer grasses, smell of overgrown grasses
The green snake cornered in the sun and stoned to
  death
Red ants swarm and lick its white belly, the smell
Above my head as I genuflect in the dizzying smell
YOU rise more and more haughtily, and tower
Your upper part, growing higher into the blue clouds
Drawn ever deeper into the middle of the clouds

To what shall I compare my god barely drowsing
In this floss of enclosing fragrant clouds?

PRICK A sleeping baby rabbit, a resting dove with its head
or HEAD   buried under the spot where its wings cross
A puppy, a kitten, a naked baby mouse
A leopard cub, a tiger cub, a wolf's babe
The Lion King's sleeping prince
A newborn lamb, its name: Innocento
Or Emmanuel, or again Salvador
A nursling among nurslings, a life among lives
An infant in the bedstraw of a stable
A solitary child wrapped in a radiate halo
An infant king who is offered tribute and felicitation
By stars, shepherds, and wise men, in other words, by
  the whole world
A horse stretches its neck toward the sleeping infant
  and neighs
As it neighs, the iron bells on its neck clank
Each of the horses that come and go along the highway
  has bells on its neck
Camel bells, mule bells, donkey bells
Bells on the ox of an ox-cart, large bells and small bells
A wayside shrine's marvelously slitted copper bell one
  clangs
Pulling the rope made of twined red and white ropes
A bell-shaped censer
The censer at the end of the chain an acolyte swings to
  the priest's litany

The censers being swung in the thousand chancels of a
thousand sanctuaries on the *duplex I classis*
On a bright summer evening the rain goddess wets the
dome of a great temple with her tongue
The mosque of Cairo, the mosque of Tripoli, the
mosque of Tunis
Hagia Sophia of Constantinople
The font of Hagia Sophia
The Tower of Babel from which the inheritors of the
earth scattered in the four directions
The giant totem pole that monkeys climb
The giant birth-stone a thousand blind men cling to
and lick
Fire worshippers' fire tower, the Oloth altar that
scorches heaven
The Altar of Heaven, the yin-yang platform, the astro-
logical tower of the doctors from the East
The dome of a great observatory, the armillary sphere
A planetarium which enwraps a faultless starry sky
An advertising tower, the barber's candy stick that
turns, an artery and vein entwining it
The scarlet knob on a bridge post, the marble statue of
an angel near the bridge
A castle fair on the hill, towers soaring in a closed city
of stone
A watchtower where a night guard paces back and
forth, rattling his gun and sword
The tower in a fort, the tower in a monastery, the tower
in the King's castle
With an innocent man incarcerated, the tower of a
ruined castle rises in deep silence
A ghastly moon out of the clouds gives half of it to
light, half of it to shadow—
A marshy zone where fog rises every night—un-
sheathing itself from the whirling flows of fog, a
tower
A finely crackled tower, a tower covered with green ivy
A tower in the wasteland, a tower in the forest, a tower
on the cliff, a lighthouse washed by waves
Pharos in ancient times burning raw olive

Flames itself bright, and only itself, in the dark sea and
the dark night—
In the morning sea, parting waves churning white, a
prideful figurehead
Sharply slicing apart the blowing ocean wind
Continues to dream of a glittering haven far beyond the
ocean route—
Sails swollen with wind, a ship swollen with sails
A battleship, a destroyer, a landing craft
A submarine moving through the depths of heavy
water
Launched incessantly upward from its nose, torpedoes
The shark-shaped torpedo, the torpedo-shaped shark
A shark, a dolphin, a sperm whale, the big fish that
swallowed the prophet
Jerked up with a cruel hook, a fish with a gleaming bel-
ly
Taken out of the fish belly, twitching entrails wet with
blood
A young fishmonger's obscene hands soiled with sticky
blood
Gleaming fish moving through the brine a thousand
fathoms deep
His nude body closely draped with corpses of noc-
tilucae
A man swims over-arm toward a boat in the offing
A slimy fur seal, a sea lion, an otter
Caught in an aurora, a seal barks on the floe
Heaven's inverse tower peering out of the unknowable
heavens
God's fingers, the miraculous fingers that give up bless-
ings
Tathagata's light-emanating fingers towering at the
limits of heaven
The thumb that the *imperator* with a sharp-eyed eagle
perched on his stout shoulder
Raises ponderously to signal "Strike!"
The fingers for the signals a catcher with powerful hips
makes between his thighs

The stonemason's sinewy thick fingers, the cooper's
    chapped fingers
A young *yakuza's* severed small finger, discolored in a
    small cloth
The philanderer's hooked, hunting finger
The toes arched toward the horizon of pleasure and
    death
Stubborn toes, willful toes, brazen, shameless toes
The shanks of Atlas indurate under the weight of
    heaven, the pillars of heaven
Marble pillars that supported the gabled roof of a pan-
    theon
Under the blue sky, columns lie shattered, now with
    nothing to support
The pillars of the Senate, pillars of a gallery surround-
    ing a plaza, pillars of the Colosseum
The Colosseum's arena, the bottom of a silence guard-
    ed by thousands of cruel eyes
The stiffened legs of contestants who yell and clash
On the dry ground, a chopped, heavy shank
In the swirling dust of a bullring, a mad blind bull
A cattle herd in a corral, a leaping bull, a bull-headed
    bull, a violent bull in rut
Battling bulls grinding their arched horns together
A drinking horn ornamented with gold work
The unicorn, the rhinoceros' unseemly horn
The velvety antlers that a young stag in early spring
    rubs against a stump itchingly
The malevolent interglacial horse, now extinct
A rushing horse, a bronco, an impetuous, spirited,
    rearing horse
A knight in the saddle, chest stuck out, armor glisten-
    ing
An advancing knight, a retreating knight, a triumphant
    knight
Neck pierced, a knight topples down
The sword a knight holds over his head, a sword that
    has been given a benediction, an emerald dagger
A decorative sword inlaid with agate and jade

38

A spear pierces a pliant youth, its spearhead upright
The red hot blade, the cutting edge of a sword, the
    blade of a hatchet, the blade of a kitchen knife
That are hammered by turns on the blacksmith's anvil
A soldering iron pulled out of charcoal fire and glowing
    fire
A burning log one pulls out of the stove, a torch in the
    dark
One sucks in, and the cigar glows
Dawn-colored ivory, the mammoth's elegantly arched
    tusk
A ruddy-faced craftsman dexterously
Pulls a long iron tube out of the molten oven
And balling up his cheeks, blows a bottle shape
A lamp in a mountain hut, a hanging-lamp in a boat
    house, a dark-lantern
The chimney of the lamp that boys of Harlem used
    night after night
To burn with its oily-smelling flames the hair of the
    parts they were bashful about
The glowworm that goes back and forth through the
    dark marrow of a tree
A silkworm, a larva, a magnificent maggot sated on
    rotten meat
A slug leaves a gleaming trail, weaving ahead
A viper with its fierce head, a rattlesnake, a slow
    python
Under a caressing hand a cobra raises its sinuous head
    for love
A tamed Indian tortoise, the tortoise's leathery head
A leathery elephant, the elephant's leathery trunk, a
    Goblin's long nose
A hooked nose, a roman nose, a snotty nose
A boxer's squashed nose, a nose dripping with a cold
A purplish nose ulcerous from liquor
A nose sniffing for the wine smell from a distant wine
    cellar
A wine jar in the wine cellar's inmost part, a milk jar, a
    jar of honey

A pigskin sack one hooks to the wall to ripen cheese in
A leather sack of wine a thirsty traveler
Takes down from his horse, holds up in both hands,
    puts his mouth to, and guzzles from
Peach-colored stuffed meat dangling in the dark of a
    butcher shop, a half-rotten ham
An abundantly seasoned, well salted, purplish-black
    sausage
As they sway greenbottles fly about noisily buzzing—
Salt pork on the carving board, a pickled cucumber, a
    pickled eggplant
An apple baked with rum, a peach baked with cognac
A leaden *pidan* that ripened in mud, a heavy egg boiled
    too long
A light peach-colored nesting egg that one makes a
    hole in with a gimlet and slurps from
A goose egg that has an erotic picture on it, painted
    with a delicate gold-covered Chinese brush
A duck egg, a turkey egg, a guinea hen's mottled egg
Fox-colored fried cookies with plenty of milk and yolk
In the crowd of an open-air market one fondly
    remembers
A fat elephant of a man, all smiles
Sprinkles sweet sugar, top and bottom
With his huge hand rubbed on his apron—
A red mullet seasoned with pepper, *wijnruit*, onion,
    and mustard
Heliogabalus' conger eels fed and fattened
On the live flesh of young slaves handpicked for brawn
    and beauty
A carp fried whole, a lamprey cooked whole
Cod roes, sea bream roes, roes of a roach crisscrossed
    with blood vessels
Pomegranates that have exploded on each branch,
    showing blood-colored insides, exploded heads
A head that ripened to the full and dropped from the
    neck, blood spurting
A criminal's head a wrestler wrenched off, his arms
    bulging with muscles

A rebel's head rolling, chagrined, under the guillotine
A boxer's neck with swollen veins, a philosopher's
    neck, Agrippa's head
A neck with two or three lines of soiled wrinkles, the
    lightly dyed neckskin
The head of a lion baring his incisors, the head of a
    foaming horse near death, a bull's bloodied head
The neck of a wild goose flying over reed marshes, a
    drake's blue neck swiftly erected
The neck of a proud fighting cock, the neck of a
    cassowary, a chicken's neck rolling on the floor of
    a poultry shop
A flower that blossomed to the full and dropped with
    its calyx, the head of a flower
And since we're on flowers, the bud of a pallid, ponder-
    ous lily
The bud of a cape jasmine, buds of a purple magnolia,
    an evergreen magnolia
An anemone about to open, moist with dew
A tulip about to open, a water lily about to open
A creeping myrtle hanging from vines, a trumpet
    creeper
An akebi torn purple, hanging from heaven
Duped by the sweet-sour fragrance, from somewhere
Slim-waisted yellow jackets gather—
A mango, papaya, durian with a strong aroma
A banana gives off fragrance when peeled
The coconut one holds with both hands in a cool shade
    and pleasantly drinks its juice from
The tight, bumpy head of a native drinking from a
    coconut
Novel fruits brought over across the salt-fragrant
    oceans
Mandarin oranges guarded by Hsi Wang Mu's ladies-in-
    waiting
Litchi nuts with a taste of tears, which messengers
    carry a thousand miles, whipping relays of horses
Monstrous nuts that speak a human tongue in a bar-
    baric Hsi-yu country
In the morning field, a dew-drenched, muddy melon

A watermelon, its red inside peering out of the crack
    made when it dropped on the road
A butchered infant's head, its wet brains peering out
Inside a sleeping infant sleeps an adult
Life in a sleeping adult, death in life
Glory equal to ruin, medicine equal to poison, good
    equal to evil
Temptation equal to salvation, salvation equal to temp-
    tation
Adam on the sixth day of creation, equal to the fallen
    archangel
The terrifying judge on the day of judgment, equal to
    one waiting at the bottom of hell's darkness
Ruler of the lights and shadows of mountains, rivers,
    and deserts
Of oceans and firmament, cities and countries
The one pierced by the arrows, *oratio jaculatoria,* of
    prayers and grudges, of ice and fire
Shot by the multitudes that merely repeat births and
    deaths
In the four directions, scanned with narrowed eyes,
    hand shading the light
To the limits of the earth where horse hoofs swirl up
    dust
The only word, the only law, the only principle—
Before YOUR dazzling self entwined with the vines
Of our adorations and curses, I shall prostrate myself
I shall weep, I shall plead, I shall entreat

There, I caught you
Lovely male rabbit
Held down in my hands, you bounce
With vigor, like a spring
Like the tip of a fountain pressed under the hand of a
    naughty boy
Like a balloon a young stallkeeper pumps hydrogen in-
    to
And then makes squeak on a festival night
Like a carp the diver in the cold February water
Has gripped with both hands
I caught you, in the dark of a newsreel theater
In the forest of human columns in a steam-filled
    Turkish bath
In the cloud of aromas in a public men's room
In the sweat-reeking throngs on a crowded train
Wait, agile male rabbit
Hopping down the stairs to the basement country
That suggests the river bank in Wonderland
Where are you running away to?

GROPETERIA Underneath is a forest of miracles
Off the busy street, in a cheap basement movie house,
    behind its empty front seats
The wordlessly stirring forest is a forest of flesh
What curse has changed these people
Into abominable trees?
Oh, these saint-like, apostle-like people
Standing uneasily, unable to move!
To the eye that has entered the dark abruptly from light
These thronging people loom merely black
But as they sway like aristae swaying
Almost imperceptibly on a windless, full moon night
Their heads, their shoulders
Blurred by the reflections of white images
Cast on the screen, are like the blessed signs
To tell holiness by, the dazzling auras
The shadows spout black sweat
Feigning indifference, but the moment the backs of
    hands casually groping
Assure each other they turn with the alacrity

Of aspen leaves in the wind, and the hunting fingers
Swim into the spaces between fingers, the parts where
    thin webs are
And in the end tightly grip each other
Hand, the first signal exchanged, separates from hand
Falls upon the stirring bulge in the cloth of the other's
    pants
And welcomes, fondles, loves
The sugar lump which, licked by ants of pleasure
Crumbles from its top in drivels blended with formic
    acid
The nest of yellow jackets full of holes
Packed with flabby delicious wasp babies
Around the encounter of two martyrs, the other saints
Happily make a firm, protecting, human fence
In which the two exchange love where a moment is an
    eternity
Here in the catacombs
There are no burning candles, shining icons, or glitter-
    ing ritual objects
But people gather here from crossroads, from net-
    works of labyrinths
With the same sufferings, same wishes, same longings
Their other secret meeting place is the place closest to
    the skies
After climbing and climbing many turns of stairs
A cheap movie house with a low ceiling that touches
    one's head
Its lavatory—the back of a building is all that's visible
    from its small window
From there, can't one go to heaven's lavatory along the
    road of an invisible rope?
At this very moment, in heaven's lavatory, among
    young angels
Are YOU dreamily jerking off?
Here, to climb is to descend
To descend, to climb
No, to climb and to descend are one
As in the Eleusinian mysteries

TURKISH
EMBASSY

Come now, wait, naughty child
What's ahead of this hole is a sacred basement Turkish
    bath
One pushes in the steamy glass door like the entrance
To limbo, and on hell's languidly descending slope
Faces blurred like soles of feet all turn to look
Noses and ears gone flabby, and near their amorphous
    eyes
Dizzying blind mirrors are plastered
One looks back, and there
At the focal distance of the lens of steam, a crowd of
    distorted ghosts
The white steam that leaks from a pipe rusted red
    spurts up
Hissing, hits the wall, changes its direction
All at once reaches the ceiling
And exhausted, drips, drips, drips
And drips onto the flowing floor where sitting flatly
Like the lion Heracles the bathhouse god once kept
Mouths smellier than the latrine, darker than the grave,
    agape
Tongues bent like a carpenter's square, just as sea
    anemones wait for a small fish
Some wait for the arrival of a lively male rabbit
As for those standing, each one of them
Like a sick frog, has a pale swollen underbelly
Leathery pointed elbows, dirty corned heels
Several long idle hairs growing from a mole near the
    shoulder
Buttocks, fleshless, skin hanging loose like a balloon
    with the air gone
Rheum exuding from the mucous suppurating corners
    of the eyes
The eyes sidewise ogle a neighbor
And then again feign utter unconcern
These garbage bags of prurience and muck
Jostle and push one another in the chamber
And from the heads of their larvae dangling in white
    hair

Toyed with by the fingertips of absurdly long mummy
    fingers
Drips withering, smelly juice
Which threads down sluggishly like the sticky stuff in
    fermented soybeans
Should, by mistake, a boy who knows nothing
Wander in, swiftly
Vines would slide out of these garbage bags
And swaddle the boy's flesh
The vines would oh ever so lightly transport it
To the pinnacle of delight, and at the pinnacle of blaz-
    ing joy
The boy's face would easily avalanche to ugly old age
And so he too would become an insidious one among
    the crowd of insidious *pretas*
In the boiling Tapana Hell
The saint's phrase, "the community of hatred"
Is appropriate for this hateful crowd
Verily, here there's no love of any kind
But it is also true that they are yearning for
A love like enwrapped light
A love enrolled in a cocoon of gentleness
Like that of the stars of the Twins
How, and where, have the tips of the lights
These travelers protected as they wandered in the land
    of love
Gone awry in storms of evil?
Saints, pity these people

TEA HOUSE The hole also leads to the public men's room under-
ground
The spiral staircase turns twice, turns three times
Excreta, semen, tar of tobacco, sodden, rotting emo-
tions
From them, furiously, rise the scents—in their midst
In the drifting five-colored clouds, in the mist of the five
skandha, one stands and strains one's eyes
The four sides of the cloud-mist painful to the eye are
the concrete walls of grief that nightly suck the
dew—
On the walls, ideograms of grief jostling, rising to the
ceiling, psalms of grief
—One of them:

Romance of the Rose

Budding rose, rose with everted petals,
dew-laden rose
My rose-shaped love, my god
Where have you gone, leaving me, aban-
doning me
Abandoned, forgotten, I have become an
idle grave
My love, asking for you, my god, looking
for you
I have gone past many crossroads, but I
have not found you
I am exhausted, both soul and flesh
I pray, you whom I love will pity me
Descend from heaven like a flood of light
and fill me—
My grave, my throat, down to my stomach

Envoy

*Wanted: A Young person. I would do
anything. My age uncertain. Please get
in touch.*

At the end of swirling choruses of innumerable
ideograms and innumerable psalms
Is a sacred door to the two holiest places, two shitting
places
One pushes in the door, squats before the john, and
there before one's eyes is the sacred hole
Wanting to see beyond it the light of paradise, or else
the darkness of hell
One puts one's eye to it, and as if to pierce the eye, a
thing thrusts out
One looks again: a red hot flesh-column, its tip flushed
with anger
A drop, hungry for love, a trembling transparent bead
of tear
Overcome with pity, one opens one's mouth in the
shape of O, wraps it with one's tongue
And the flesh, the spearhead, gathering strength,
thrusts out and out
Soon the taut flesh bursts, melts away
And the visitor from the other side, a god, dies
Now the one on this side stirs
Becomes a god, visits beyond the hole the wet hot
darkness
Becomes wrapped by the darkness, squeezed and
rubbed by the darkness, climbs to the top
And the god this side, too, has at once a headlong fall
Two columns of deity leave each other, and only the
hole remains, black
Verily, praise be to the hole into which one peers,
which is peered into—
Through the hole that makes two solitudes one
Two shitting places one, the public men's room leads
to the men's room of a gymnasium
Leads to the men's rooms of a fish market, a seamen's
school, the self-defense forces, a prison
A dormitory, a police academy, and a police booth
Thus one would go through the peep-hole of the public
men's room
Sneak into the men's room of a police booth, hold a
cop from behind

48

Tie up his hands on his back, take off his belt, pull
   down the zipper
Drop his pants, hug his hips tight
And make him arch back with pleasure, make him
   groan, writhe
And die in spasms—oh all those young, sturdy cops
Even among them, among those thousands and
   thousands of illusory cops
YOU are not found

the PRICK,　Night, with downy hair trembling the color of gold, em-
again　　　braces
A pure sleep, a pure spirit, a pure substance
For example, pure gold, silver, iron ore
Light dug out of the dark earth: diamond
Muddy crystal columns, amethyst, garnet
A pure idea, a pure poem, a pure death
Its innocent mimesis
Like the soft roe which, taken out of the pliant belly
Of a leaping male salmon gleams a rainbow color
Like the corpse of a drowned boy rising from the water
In the arms of sorrowful water nymphs
Like the ancient bronze statue of a god which the
   wordless divers
Tie to a rope and haul up from the bottom of the sea
You, glistening-wet, inert
Keep falling, or keep climbing
Into a heavier sleep, into a deeper sleep—
BUSH　　Surrounding a sleeping, parentless, infant brother, and
   shining
Are his elder sisters—like their lice-infested hair
Surrounding you in sleep, and shining
Are a water nymph of the sea, a water nymph of the
   river
Water nymphs of the marshes, of the waterfall, of the
   spring, their hair
The hairs of the sea that waver as the tides move
Rockweed, kelp, thick-haired codium, gulfweed
Various duckweeds, in bright fresh water

A flock of reeds at the estuary quivers delicately
When ebbing tides cry out in the evening sun
A marshy zone where a murderous felon escaped
A thicket of ferns where a phallus, rotted purple, lies
    abandoned
A field of bamboo grass, a field of sedge,
A neatly mowed lawn
A well-groomed brushwood fence
On a moonlit night, a farm hand riding a donkey
    sidesaddle
Plays the flute, passes by a field of sweet-smelling
    sugar cane
A reindeer fawn, left behind by its mother
Sad-eyed, sniffs its way over the steppe
Hungry hyenas roam the savanna
A wounded lion hides in a thicket of tall grass
A hot wind passing through the thicket
Fans out burnt grasses, insects, and the shrill smell of
    blood—
A hedgerow of roses where a snake hides, a bramble of
    thorns
On the cool inner wall of a well in the country moss
    thrives
A green forest in fragrant May
In the soft sun that filters through the trees
Students on the wrestling team, sitting back to back
Arms hooked, legs stretched
Push and pull, by turns, to strengthen abdominal
    muscles
Oh, how they resemble those making love—
One summer day, and the cool foliage of a
    honeysuckle
In which two cute boys loved
Each other, cooing like two doves
In the heat of the day, Indian travelers, like persons in
    meditation
Rest with eyes closed in the shade of a linden
There's a yogurt vender with Indian cotton wound
    around his head—
There's a cow sacred to the gods, relaxing leisurely,

four legs tucked under its body—
Brats playing at soldiers
Hide in bushes of plume goldenrod, stiff goldenrod,
      wasteland aster—
The day when the inner sides of one's thighs become
      sweaty, while marsh wrens jar
A golden wheat field—crawling into it
A young man makes a blushing boy play with him
The boy is moved, his heart beating like a fire bell—
July's gentle green paddies, paddies of rush
On a rafter, premonitions of a storm make a swallow
      chick tremble—the down on its neck
On a wind-howling night, heaths on the slope abruptly
      turn pale
A stormy forest, a shadowy forest, the King of the
      Wood's forest
—Here again the season of a fragrant forest
The demons' metropolis, the forest with rows of giant
      trees that stab heaven
During the day, young mothers pushing baby carriages
Grandmothers plying knitting needles, girls reading
Mischievous children in short pants, gentle lovers
Fill a corner—a heartwarming sight—
Which, as dusk sets in, reveals the other face of Janus
And in the shadows of trees, around the fence of roses,
      men begin to loiter
Their eyes flare, twinkling in the dark
Like the phosphorescence around a bone on a rainy
      night
These blue phosphorescent lights, sluggishly flaring
Draw large slow circles
And, each turning into viscous lime, pull each other
      closer
The hunter and the hunted—the movements of the two
      circles
Gradually slow down and finally stop
The phosphorescent lights that have become one, still
      smoldering
In due time leave somewhere

Two a.m., three a.m.
The forest still fragrant, circles still drawn
And soon the eastern clouds whitening

PRICK
and BALLS A foundling wrapped in gentle feathers
The she-wolf with the twins, Romulus and Remus
Acala the god of fire attended by Kimkara and Cetaka
Tathagata flanked by his warriors
A cannon with its two wheels
A rocket launcher equipped with two hangars—
From which the deaths of men will be recorded in a
giant log of the space age
Are launched one after another—
A carriage with two impetuous horses
The sacred triangle, Ugolino weeping with his starved
sons
Youngest prince Okuninushi carrying sacks on his
back
BALLS Bag of wrinkled leather as old as the world
A bag of tears, a bag of placer gold, a bag of sorrows of
pure gold
A heavy purse of supremely soft deerskin
Filled out with jingling gold coins
Wrinkles at its mouth collected and tightly tied
A brocaded bag with flints in it
A terrifying matchbox crammed with dangerous
matches
An amulet bag, a sachet, a silk napkin with a famous
incense folded in it
On Christmas Eve, Santa Claus flies through the
aurora
His cloth sack full of goodies
Decorating the four corners of an old leather map, the
wind gods with their windbags
Momotaro's waist pouch bulging with delicious millet
dumplings
Seasonal laborers looking for new jobs

Tramp along the dusty road, shoulders burdened with canvas bags

In a boxing gym, a boy attacks and sways a punching bag

Two weights, a balance

Hermes' snake-coiling balance with hefty gold lumps in both pans

In the golden year of a bumper crop, wine barrels are laid

Solidly filling the dim basement cellar

One puts in a ladder, goes down

And loses one's foothold, blunted by the mist of sweet-sour smell—

One peers in, and the oil in the jar wavers slimily

Tangled by spiders' slime, an endplate exudes

White dregs from its crack, of a sturdy barrel of Vino de Jerez

An iced-over pond on the mountaintop

On a bitterly cold night, the pond keeper spikes his fierce pick in

And the gallant water, spouting out as light

Jumps over the icicle-hung watergate, and comes down shrieking—

A frozen dragon egg, salmon roe embossed with blood vessels

In the water, a hyacinth bulb embossed with purple veins

The narcissus, the crocus, the saffron with their pinkish bulbs

A bunch of grapes, ripe and heavy, mulberries ripe in a foliage

A dew-laden cluster of genista flowers

A flower cluster of wisteria, paulownia flowers heavy with last night's rain

Drooping ears of millet moving in the wind, golden ears of rice in October

The deep sea that nourishes pearls, fish eggs laid on laver brushwood

A dragnet at the bottom of dark water, heavy before it is drawn up

A thunderhead, a cloud pregnant with light, a raincloud
enfolding a whole town
An uninhabited house on a stormy day, the hideout of
a murderer
A fortress with its drawbridge lifted, the miracle palace
concealing villains
The closed Pentagon, the silent G.P.U. headquarters
In a wasted village, a towering belfry
Where for joy, or for sorrow
Innumerable bells of yore are ringing—
A blast furnace, a retort, a percolator
A thermal power plant in the folds of the mountains, a
highly fragrant bread oven
The pot-maker's oven, in the depths of its fire master-
pieces ripening
On a stormy night a thrushes' nest thumps down to the
ground, clamorous chicks and all
A mischievous child pulls out from under a tree root
A trapdoor spider's nesting bag with the spider squirm-
ing in it
Sloshily moving, a rubber waterpillow
Folding on a rainy day and opening when it's clear, the
pine cone
A slow rhinoceros with straggling hair, the leathery
rhinoceros the leather bag
When it looks as if it's moving, it's quite still
And when it looks still, it's moving—a loose leather-
made ball
Folded in a well-tanned, gentle sheepskin, a thick book
of wisdom

54

As an infant, tiptoe, touches with its lovely hand
A loaded cluster of grapes wet with morning dew
As a forbidding mountain exorcist, whose traveling
   robe is of hemp
Worries and rustles his rosary of coarse beads in his
   terrifying hands
So one worries the balls in one's hands
Kisses the child wrapped in the wrapping cloth

FORESKIN

And with the tongue tip sharpened like a needle, everts
   the wrapping cloth
A bandage wound tightly round and round the ring
   finger
The bandages for an abscess, the bandages rolling up
   a fireman burned all over
The bandages that wrap the invisible man, the band-
   ages with a mummified boy-king sleeping in them
The white cover-cloth a leper has pulled over himself,
   from head to toe
The flowering stalk of a butterbur, a peapod, skin-
   covers of a bamboo shoot
A miscanthus roll, a taffy in a bamboo leaf, a butterball
   wrapped in cellophane
A hat, the Pope's miter, a cardinal's hat, the hood for a
   child in the snow country
The chef's somewhat grimy white toque
The K.K.K. hood, socks, a rubber thimble
A rubber glove everted like a pelt of gelatin
A god's glove that has fallen from heaven toward the
   sea of chaos
A turban, a calpac, the hood of the Eskimo parka
Roofs rising in the Kremlin, in rows as if in a fairy tale
In the Kremlin, from the balcony
Soviet elders wave to May Day crowds in Red Square
All in uniform caps
At Buckingham Palace, guards swagger in bearskins
Pericles' helmet, Napoleon's hat
The Pohai Emperor's hat, the Egyptian priest's head-
   dress
The Old Blossomer's cap, Mr Ebisu's cap

The fearful shoes, the shoes that, once put on, can't be
removed
The rubber boots worn by a young cock in the fish
market
The riding boots made to fit the legs closely
Each time the rider walks its spurs clack, clack
A hill-fresh yam wearing a maxicoat
A wandering yakuza's slightly soiled cape
A man rolled in a mattress carried by thugs to be
dumped in the river
One unhooks the beltless, pulls the zipper
And recklessly pulls down the pants
A gaiter unwound swiftly, the leather chaps
A shutter pulled down with a rattle, a curtain, a double-
leaf louver door
Concealing a man, panting, his hairy shins showing, a
surgical intern in white
A noncommissioned officer's cap pulled down to the
eyes, his uniform well-creased
The armor hiding the young blond knight, his Lordship
On a morning when each exhaled breath visibly turns
into steam, white misty droplets
An auto repairman's one-piece workwear
The zipper extending down its stained cloth from neck
to crotch
When one pulls it down in one breath
There, vividly, jumps out the young flesh, flushed with
cold—
The leaping pink flesh wrapped in a lobster shell
The pelty diving suit, a suede suit
Skinned with a stone and bloody, a wild animal pelt
An antelope, a wolf, a coyote, their pelts
The membrane that wraps the bloody heart of a wild
animal
The membrane of the morning haze that wraps the
bloody daybreak

CHEESE

When one rolls up the haze, the gossamer tent
Soaked with morning dew is the refreshing sun
Brilliant scum around the sun
Corona, halo, ring around the eclipsed sun
On the triumphant soldier's forehead, a hoop of young
    laurel, olive and myrtle branches
A crown for breaking blockades, a citizens' crown, a
    naval crown, a crown on the castle wall
The ecliptic, the headband, that holds the celestial
    globe at an angle
The equatorial belt, heaven's band of animals, its
    twelve palaces
Saturn's double rings, the sash of Iris the rainbow god-
    dess
The turquoise pectoral of Tutankhamon the boy king
The pectoral of gold plates that shine in many layers
Adjective, adverb, and again adverb that adorns the
    adverb
Dazzling rhythms around true poetry
Appoggiaturas that hold on to the *Idee* of a great sym-
    phony
Gentle compassion around true strength
Thoughtfulness, delicacy, salt of the earth
Ashes that dye the brows on Ash Wednesday
Ashes of the hemp ropes burnt on the felicitous morn-
    ing of the election of a new Pope
Paste perfume, balsam, musk, ambergris
Cheese the northerners stir and ripen in goatskin bags
Honey congealed, fragments of a shell on which glue
    was kneaded
An island of mew gulls
The birds nesting along the round rim of the rocky isle
Fly away north leaving the rock mountain
Encircled by a necklace of dry white bird shit—
A white town cradling a bay, a full set of false teeth
A round archipelago, a ring of coral reefs—now, the
    tongue's violent storm
Is about to lap up the whole atoll, look
When the tongue slurps past

CREVASSE
and
CHORDEE

The furrow opens joyfully, the furrow leading to the
    cord
A string twisting together innumerable gold fibers of
    pleasure
An electric cord through which run a thousand am-
    peres of joy
A Japanese lute's resonating string, a "demoncalmer's"
    trembling bowstring
A purling stream of groans, a gleaming channel marker
A quaking arc of light, a platinum sheet of rain, a silver
    blind
Lightning, a road arrested in lightning
A bright sea line, an unmarked sea boundary
A horizon fringed by light
From over an invisible line, on horseback, on
    camelback
Or on foot, new toiling races
Emerge, one after another—
The most sensitive barometer thread
The breathtaking galactic belt
Over a dizzying gorge a taut suspension bridge
And again, the sway of the tongue
Provokes around the furrow a chorus of roars from the
    millet grains of pleasure
The sun pours its light on a single plate
In the bullring, and in the arena
Seeing blood the spectators resound in fury
The faithful congregate in the Vatican on Easter
School children at the command, "Line up for exer-
    cises!"
A thousand soldiers on review, at the moment of "Pre-
    sent arms!"
A thousand black slaves on the boy-king's august visit
The tongues of barnacles swing in unison at each move
    of the tide
On the late summer sea a thousand ripples, a thousand
    staysails
A thousand fragments of the evening sun on the
    lake—oh YOU

58

Please stick your praiseworthy head out of the shatter-
ing water—
A thousand zelkova leaves all sway at once
A flock of starlings fly up clamorously
In the United States of America, on Independence Day
And in the Soviet Union, on Revolution Day
Planes in a large formation converge, scatter, and then
again converge
On the belt of a cultured-pearl factory hurry billions of
pearls. . . .

Eightfold camellia that flowers on my tongue full of
love
Droplets of honeydew that collect at the tip of a petal
Drops of costly perfumed oil that tremble on the alem-
bic
FORECOME Thrust forward by thoughts of tender love, I press my
and COME lips
To the camellia, to the alembic, to the wide-mouthed
jar
Joyous glitter
That spouts and goes down my throat into hell
Frothy honey liquor that brims over the wide-mouthed
pot
And spills along the shapely furrow, leaving a gleaming
trail
Way beyond the seas of waves tossing in winter
storms
Ferocious barbarians of an unknown country
Brewed and stored it through seasons of lasting fog
and hail
The men who brewed it are gutsy and rough
But the liquor that was born is smooth and gentle to
the tongue—
The sacred water that wells up on Oceanus' purifying
island
And is carried in the beak of a sapient dove
To Olympus, to the lips of the gods

Dr. Faustus' mercury, the spirit of the mercury-colored
    earth
The water that courses through the dark underground
    paths
A deep well one crackles by dropping a bucket on a
    dark night
A sudden spout in a winter park
The smoke a rocket spews
Viscous fumes from a volcano
Lava that dribbles down toward the mountain foot
Time that drips, a clepsydra
An avalanche, a glacier going down
Frozen waterfalls, icicles, frost columns
Firefly's saliva to feed its larvae
Dragon's slobber, snake's tears, slug's path
Saint James' way, the milky river made when heaven's
    giant vat was overturned
In heaven, Ganymede the beautiful boy coyly pours
    nectar
From a wide-mouthed *krater*
A shooting star, a shower of the starry host
Billions of well-washed pearls
Billions of incessant arrows
Sidelong glances, a row of arrows
Darts of light, arrows of words
Love God's arrows that escape the mouth of a boy in
    love
a krim namah. . . .
A swarm of honey bees, the sharp spring messenger
    the *Kokila* bird
Light, Holy Spirit, the tongue of a flame going down
    noisily
A delighted spring, a joyful stream
Touched by light, Persephone's water cries out happily
At midnight, a water-surprise
On a festival night, fireworks
A sudden visit
Brightly between the thighs, angels
The Word, what is eternally sonlike, overflows

Cheerfulness, innocence, directness comes forth
But hold it, hold it
Frowning, lips closed
And repeat over and over
Making no sense, the changes of a verb:
I will *not* fly
I *will* fly
I fly
When I fly
If I flew
Fly
Let me fly
Let's fly!

GET YOUR   Childhood dream of flying through space
ROCKS OFF   Tom Thumb riding a goose
Eleven princes who turned into swans
Clever kids lifted to a star
Star-shaped confetti
Confetti, alfeloa shots
Shots to blind the enemy in a snowball fight
Bow-and-arrow fight, Lord Protector of Bows and Ar-
rows, arrows numbering eighty thousand
Hundreds and thousands of stones flipped from a
catapult
An artillery, an anti-aircraft gun, machine gun strafe
like hailstones
In a kids' war, a shower of pebbles
A knapsack hurled off
Textbooks thrown out, cards
Heaven's jewelry box thrown out
Angels who flew away
Heaven's forces on birds' wings
Hell's army on bats' membranes
A great space war that weaves through the stars
A great formation that falls burning
Dandelions parachute
Pollen that flies up in the wind
Golden kerria roses that scatter in the wind

Kerria King's generous treat
Cakes scattered, bags scattered to the crowd
Scattering large coins, small coins
Scatter, scattering away
Rolling up like a fetus
Headfirst, headlong
Heavy, lonesome, fall!

BALLAD FOR Ah, where are they?
THE LONG- In what netherworld
DEAD BOYS Is that strange soldier who one flaming night of air raid
Picked me up
And pressed his cheek to mine?
As he picked me up
My young cheeks rubbed against the thighs of his
    soldier pants
And hurt pleasantly
And where are
Those handkerchiefs hung from the hips
Of the drafted students who went past me
Turning back, again and again
To see me playing with mud?
Those young fishermen
Who on starry nights, in the ship-carpenter's hut
Taught us the suffocating pain of dirty stories?
Those railway men
Out of whose faded, dark-blue work clothes
Bruised youth peered?
And yet, where are they?
Where are the roses of yesteryear?

Ah, where are they?
Under what sky
Are those cruel upper graders
Wearing shorts, knees showing?
Those bullies who on the way home from school
Ambushed me in the shrine wood
And sank me
In fond dizzying noseblood?
And where is

That junior high school gymnast
Who did a giant swing, turned round and round
Not deigning to glance at me
An admiring, spellbound schoolboy?
Or those vagrant kids who stole
The black puppy I loved so?
Mother went and pleaded with them
And obediently they returned it—their sad eyes?
And yet, where are they?
Where are the lilies of yesteryear?

For those kings, those cheerful princes
Do not ask where they are
Their youth, those mornings
Those flesh-colored mists and showers
They are all gone, leaving not a trace
And yet, and yet
Where are the flowers of yesteryear?

Where are YOU? Where have you gone?
I'll go out to search
Who are you? Who, really?
Among whom have you been lost?
Among the crowd of lonely men who fill the town
When day's magnificent downfall dyes heaven and
    earth?
Among the men cramming the lighted trains hurrying
    through the underground network of labyrinths?
Among the men jerking off in a single row, in the
    spacious men's room of a terminal?
Among the men shooting balls, ass to ass, in the
    perspective of a *pachinko* hall?
Among the men downing cups of sake, at a sake-
    storefront?
Among the braves marching zigzag, in helmets, with
    wood poles?
Among the warriors in Duralumin head-pieces and
    Duralumin shields?

Among the yakuza in *dabo* shirts? Among the tough
guys with tattoos of Krikara the dragon king?
Among the young men at the festival wearing nothing
but plain loincloths under short coats?
Chimney sweeps, plasterers, hard-hats
Killers, gangsters, bosses of the underworld
Blood-splattered slaughterers, blood-splattered
fishmongers
A surgeon proud of his brawn, freshly, terrifically
shaven
A singer with his bumptious throat, legs arched on the
stage
Robber drivers of the dump trucks that speed in a
string along night's highway
Pig iron handlers made of the same stuff as the iron
burning in the blast furnace
Coal miners with their lighted heads, stark naked gold
mine workers
Negro laborers in a diamond mine
The Minotaur in a dungeon, a centaur in a fury
A guardsman in a sealed bank who comes and goes
like clockwork through the night
A diver who comes out of the heavy tide into light and
painfully breathes
An oily-smelling crewman on the ocean route, sweaty-
smelling fishermen off Las Palmas
A racing driver ablaze, at the moment of crashing to
death into the car ahead
Boxers bathed in blood, hugging each other
Wrestlers mimicking love-making
Bank robbers, intelligence agents, guerrillas
Revolutionaries, stolidly silent communists
The Nazi Schutzstaffel, mounted policemen, soarers
through the sky riding horses bareback
Ones who are on heaven's crossbeam, chest held high
Youths alive like stars
Young dead who have turned into stars in heaven

64

the MAN,
again

And you
Thinker astride a toilet, elbow on knee
And chin rested on palm
The thinking, powerful chin
With the flesh thrusting up, cloven in two
Lips tightly closed, knotted at the ends
Deep philtrum, nose wings breathing like an accordion
Dark nostrils, the hairs thriving in them
Swollen eyelids, shadows cast by the lowered eyelash-
  es
Thick eyebrows pulled together, making a vertical
  groove like a deep scar
And the weight on all these, the forehead
Sorrow, sufferings, love, the whole of your history
At the harsh top of you, thinking
Smoldering in morning haze, your entire thought
That is, your head, a globe
Packed with your purple many-folded brain
Is equal in value to the other brains down under you,
  thinking
Responsible for procreation, many-folded, smoldering
  in evening haze
In the thorny shrub of gleaming wire and frizzy nettles
Equal to the gizzards of wisdom
Dangling ponderously, now exposed
For the briefs are slipped from the hairy thighs down to
  the knees
The ceaseless waves of joys and of sufferings
Which, rising from your hidden, sacred center
Cannot be caught by the naked eye
Make every muscle-path blaze fleetingly
Mounting onslaughts on both brains, above and below
Your gigantic, solitary image which is at the admirable
  center
Of all phenomena, all celestial bodies, all universes
Has, clinging to its stout neck
Its bulging shoulders, and its monolithic loins
All the pagan gods, all the holy spirits, and boys
You, who are at the venerable center of all

While seated on the toilet
Form the median point of the cross-shaped mysterious
    toilet floor
And the cross shape cut off with you, thinking
Goes under, creaking heavily
Into the dark earth, into the invisible red inside
You, who go under, who are power and are wisdom
You, who are gentleness, heaviness, and pureness
You, who are at the blazing center of all—who are
    you?
You, who are god of my gods, are NOWHERE
You on the cross-like toilet floor
Whom I have made up in my painful faith, are NO ONE
Ah!

Ode: *Afterword*

1

I once heard about a weird man from three persons each unknown to the other. The following is an image of the man I have restored by complementing from other sources the stories I heard separately:[1]

About fifty. Height, a little shorter than average. Face poorly featured and dress shabby. He always holds in his arm an ancient, black leather case—he doesn't *carry* it, he holds on to it as if it were the most precious thing he owned. How he gets his income—no matter; every day, he appears at five fixed places at five fixed hours. The five places are all cheap movie theaters which are either on the top floors or in the basements[2] of buildings in fairly busy towns not far from the center of Tokyo. He must get to these theaters by changing subways and streetcars many times. At each theater, he stands in front of the box office at a fixed time, buys a ticket, and goes in.

The man, with the ticket stub, does not go where the seats are, but directly to the men's room, goes in one of the toilet compartments—always the second from the right[3]—and locks himself in. Then, while still holding his old case, he unhooks its latch and takes out a screw driver. With the case held between his thighs, he puts the tip of the screw driver on the partition wall to the right. A close look will reveal a square board, made of the same wood as that of the wall, screwed to it at the four corners. The man carefully unscrews the screws, removes the board, takes out a similar board from his case, and fastens it with the same screws to the place where the first board was. Then he puts his case and the board just removed on his lap, and crouches. In no time, from the center of the newly fastened board, suddenly, an erect, magnificently taut penis pokes out. The man, in his crouched position, leans on the wall, takes the penis in his mouth, and pumps his head. When this has been done several times, the orignal board is put back where it was, and the man leaves the theater.

Viewed from the opposite, i.e., from the toilet compartment on the right side, this odd replacement board looks like this: at its center is an infantile graffito of the vulva,[4] with the words ENTER HERE below it, written in an equally clumsy hand. The center of the vulva is, quite thoughtfully, perforated, and attached in this hole is a piece of sponge split at the center. His business done, the compartment user, puzzled by the graffito, puts his penis in the hole, just for the fun of it; the penis goes through the sponge, and the moment it comes out in the air, it is held in lukewarm, wet flesh. After fifty to sixty dizzying seconds, the user leaves in utter confusion. The next user comes in, sees, and puts his in. . . .

These weird, living walls came in due time to be known to the managers of the theaters, and were rebuilt one after another with mineral materials. Since then, no one has seen the man. Just as the animals deprived of their environments become extinct,[5] so perhaps this man, deprived of the environment in which he could live to his liking, has also perished.

2

Who is this mysterious man? That is the subject to be explored in our essay.

In the course of our patient exploration, we discover a figure resembling our protagonist in a light verse by a modern English poet.[6] The poem, titled "Glory-hole," goes as follows:

> Loneliness sits
> In the toilet,
> Waiting for
> Reality
> To enter through the
> Glory-hole.

"Loneliness" squats on the "floor of opprobrium," waiting for the arrival of "the real" through the "holy hole of glory." The glory-hole is the hole from which, in the religious allegories dating back to the Middle Ages, the supernatural[7] is supposed to emerge.

The poet has drawn two optical lines inclining in opposite directions, with the holy hole of *The Golden Legend*[8] as the focus, and placed on one line *loneliness* as a person who sees, and on the other, *reality* as an image that is seen. These two words acquire two different meanings, depending upon whether they approach "glory-hole" or "toilet." As they approach the glory-hole, loneliness comes to mean "the infinitely lonely being," i.e., one who prays as a sinner, and reality

68

"the only thing that exists," i.e., the supernatural. As they approach the toilet, loneliness comes to mean a "male homosexual,"[9] and reality, a naked penis.

The two meanings are analogically related,[10] and the relation between "one who sees" and "one who is seen," with reality as the focus, becomes the relation between one who prays and a male homosexual and that between the supernatural and the penis. And in this case as well, the light or heavy weight in one or the other pan of the balance[11] determines the direction of the power of the two. If the prayer and the supernatural go toward the male homosexual and the penis, that is from heaven toward the earth, a descending direction.[12] If the male homosexual and the penis go toward the prayer and the supernatural, that is from the earth toward heaven, an ascending direction.[13]

Since the poet belongs to earth, it is natural that he should be committed to the ascending direction. This is an approach known as "sacred pornography"[14]. . . . Having come thus far, we begin to grasp who our protagonist really is: the protagonist of "sacred pornography," who must be viewed as a point ascending from the earth to heaven.

3

We have seen that both *loneliness* and *reality* include heaven in their meanings. Now we must realize that there are, further, an essential heaven and earth with the glory-hole at the center. Where the one who sees[15] is, i.e., this side of the glory-hole, is the earth, and where the one who is seen is, i.e., that side of the glory-hole, is heaven.[16] To take a pornographic approach, the male homosexual, the prayer, waits eagerly for the visitation of the penis, the supernatural, through the holy hole, i.e., for the visitation of the heavenly to the earthly.[17]

Under this circumstance, the only action possible for the prayer = male homosexual is to "wait,"[18] and "waiting," in the extreme of its passivity, comes to acquire an incomparably active quality. To see this point in further detail, let us explore the essence of the glory-hole.

The glory-hole is a *hole*, a void. Here, however, void is, to paraphrase Lao Tzu, "that which is useful for *what is there* (= substance) by not being there."[19] Without this void, reality, or substance, cannot enter. Furthermore, the void is not only the essence of the glory-hole; it is also the essence of loneliness, which is on this side of the glory-hole. "An infinitely lonely being" is no more than another name of "a being that is void." A "being that is void" is, of course, self-contradictory, but the self-contradiction, "He is void; therefore, he is there," is the essence of man.

The imperfect being which "is there because it is void" inevitably wills to complement the void with substance in order to become a "being that is *substantial.*" This will to be infinitely active by being infinitely passive is the act of "waiting."

To go a step further, the *most* void part of the void human being is perhaps neither vagina nor rectum, but the oral cavity.[20] For proof, suffice it to remember that the oral cavity is the only desire-fulfilling organ during Freud's so-called labial period,[21] i.e., the golden age in which the two desires, for food and for sex, are yet to be specialized. This golden age in our personal history precisely corresponds to the golden age in the history of mankind, the age of imitative magic in which procreation and fertility were the same.[22] As a result, in those churches where our two golden ages still survive,[23] the food for spirit, i.e., the sacred body of Christ, enters from the mouth, and the food for flesh, i.e., bread, water, and fish,[24] also enters from the mouth. Indeed, blessed be "that which goeth into the mouth"![25]

Thus it will be understood that our protagonist, who crouches on a toilet floor, eagerly waits for the penis that visits from the hole on the wall, and fills his oral cavity with it, is typical of the human being who "is there because he is void," "aims to be there because he is void," and "tries to be active in the passivity of waiting."

4

For our protagonist, what is the penis that visits through the hole on the wall?

The owner of the penis is not known to him. In other words, the penis is a gift of the "other side," of paradise, of the dark, of the UNKNOWN GOD—it is the Word in the shape of a dove.[26]

The Word, which is "without form, color, or weight," comes from the Father, who is the only *jitsuyu,* or "that which has substance." But when it appears before us, the *hiyu,* or "that which has no substance," the Word cannot help assuming a form because the hiyu are "with form, color, and weight." Only in this sense can "the Word was made flesh"[27] and "incarnation" be talked about. Just as for the faithful,

Christ is "the son of the Father," so for our protagonist, the penis in Japanese is the "little man" or the "son" of the jitsuyu.[28] To know that the penis is the "little man" of the jitsuyu, one has only to remember that through this part the earth continues to be inherited.

To pay for the assumption by the jitsuyu of the form of a penis, our protagonist, who is a hiyu, loses his form. In receiving a penis, he opens his mouth in the shape of O[29]—a declaration of self-renunciation that he has turned himself completely into a void before the jitsuyu, into a plastic mold[30] to perfectly accommodate its shape.

The mold of the jitsuyu is the alchemist's melting pot, otherwise known as the golden egg, which turns the penis into the Son. And the egg is the Phoenician zero, and zero the mother of all numbers, i.e., of fate.[31] It is superfluous to add that zero is one with the Phoenician letter O. Our protagonist becomes the mother of all, i.e., the vessel of the jitsuyu, by turning himself into zero.

A question remains: How could a flesh-column, which is nothing but the pathway for urine, be the incarnation of the Word? How could the basest part of the human body become the most exalted one?[32] For this question, it should suffice to remember that in the ritual in which the basest become the most exalted is manifested the profundity of the supernatural blessings. Thus the Word that was incarnated in the womb of a nameless Jewish woman was lifted to heaven through the most abominable punishment: crucifixion.

Our protagonist, allegorically, corresponds to this Jewish woman, who said, "according to thy word."[33] And she is not the only person who has to answer, "according to thy word;" as Gertrud von Le Fort says,[34] the human being, regardless of sex, must remain a woman before what is eternally male: the supernatural. And our protagonist is representative of the human being.

5

It is time we gave our protagonist an appropriate name.

Looking around, we find, most immediately, the word "homosexual." A little thought reveals, however, that in a strict sense the word has nothing *substantial*. In the correct sense of the word, *homosexual* points to a self-preservation of purity through the copulation of two homogeneous entities. And yet, basically, copulation is not homogeneous, and therefore, self-preservation of purity through it is impossible. Copulation requires a relation akin to that of the "bolt and nut," and when both participants in copulation are bolt-like beings, one of them would have to become nut-like.[35]

We have already said that not the rectum, but the oral cavity, plays the role of the nut; this is borne out by the statistics compiled by sexologists.[36] The copulative organs for male homosexuals are generally not penis/rectum, but penis/oral cavity.

That granted, we should, in the manner of Dedekind's postulate, be able to divide male homosexuals into the penis type and oral cavity type; i.e., those who receive fellatio, and those who perform fellatio. (Here it must be pointed out that the one who performs fellatio must not so much simply kiss the penis, as suck it in and fill the void of one's oral cavity with the entire bulk of the penis.)

The penis-sucker must be far more *essential* than the penis-sucked. For the one who has his penis sucked has no inevitable reason for having it done,[37] whereas the penis-sucker, because of his being as a void, inevitably relates to penis-sucking.[38] The penis-sucker, just like Eros in one of the stories in Greek mythology,[39] yearns for the penis, i.e., substance, because he is void.[40] In this sense, he ought to be called a "phallus worshipper," or a *penisist*. When we realize further that he represents the *void* human being with his *void* oral cavity, we would agree that he shall be called by the more general name of *homo-penisistus*.

So now, finally, it has become clear who our protagonist is. He is not only most human with his yearning deep "out of the abyss" and his patient act away from the eyes of the people; he is also a "hidden prayer," a saint as a point moving from the earth toward heaven.

If he is, his poor-featured and shabby-dressed being is no longer seen because, may we say, his impeccable virtuousness recognized by the supernatural, he has been lifted to heaven, the other side of the glory-hole.

---

1. A participant in a salvation rite cannot be simply inconspicuous. His inconspicuousness must also be exaggerated.

2. Here, the top floor of a building corresponds to the place closest to heaven, such as Mount Sinai, and the basement to the catacombs of early Christians.

3. Man has a tendency to go rightward. Our protagonist, in his ingrained humbleness, chooses not the compartment on the extreme right, but one next to it, to the left.

4. Imagine the Papuan symbol resembling the sun.

5. Consider, for example, the habitat problems that the Japanese crested ibis has faced in recent years; one of the family of birds exalted in the hieroglyphics of ancient Egypt, it is near extinction.

6. W.H. Auden.

7. The UNKNOWN GOD (Acts 17:23) is here called the supernatural.

8. See the double meaning of 'gold.' As noted by Freud, hoarding of gold relates to retaining of feces. See also Norman Brown.

9. As will be made clear later, the use of this term is temporary.

10. In the world of poetry it must be possible to establish a formula: Two analogical entities are of equal value.

11. That is, whether they approach the glory-hole or toilet.

12. God's direction.

13. Man's direction.

14. Etymologically, "pornography" means "writing about prostitutes." The prostitute was originally a sorceress, therefore, sacred.

15. The original meaning of *visionnaire* must be "one who peeks into heaven."

16. Heaven is eternally "the other side."

17. Man does not visit heaven; heaven visits man.

18. To "wait" is one of man's three great virtues. See Yukio Mishima, *Utsukushii hoshi.*

19. Lao Tzu, *Tao Te Ching,* Eleventh Chapter.

20. The vagina, the rectum, and the hand shaped into a round tube for onanism are all attempts to imitate the oral cavity.

21. Sigmund Freud, *Three Contributions to the Theory of Sex.*

22. In origin, the material thing imitates its image. See James George Frazer, *The Golden Bough.* Consider also the origin of grain in the Japanese *Kojiki* (Record of Ancient Matters), in which Ohogetsuhimenokami produces five types of grain from the apertures of her anatomy.

23. Roman Catholic and Greek Orthodox.

24. The Sermon on the Mount.

25. Matthew 15:11.

26. Guillaume Apollinaire (the "angelic" poet), "La Colombe."

27. John 1:14.

28. Colloquialism is often metaphysical.

29. As in "O my darling" and "O my God."

30. A *super*mold, that is.

31. Consider numerology and expressions such as "His days are *numbered.*"

32. Herein lies the secret universal to all religions.

33. Luke 1:38. To translate, "according to the size of your magnificent equipment."

34. Gertrud von Le Fort, *Die ewige Frau.*

35. The principle of complement, applicable to relations such as that between the butch type and the nelly type.

36. For example, Albert Moll, *Die homosexuelle Liebe.*

37. Being human, he has no necessity to become God.

38. "God is what comes from behind us." See Ranier Maria Rilke, *Das Studenbuch.* Also, as a Japanese proverb goes, "The sardine's head is what you believe it to be."

39. See Plato, *The Symposium.*

40. Consider the cannibalism in the Mass. Christ Himself said that He was bread sent from heaven (Luke 22:19). Also, male homosexuals "eat" to fulfill their desire.

from

SELF-PORTRAITS 50

(1965-1974; published 1975)

Myself with a Hand Holding a Pen

The nails of a beautiful healthy hand should be dawn-colored, aga-
toid,
like any part of a celestial globe, perfectly spherical, marvelously
arched,
from the horizon of each nail a clear-cut half-moon peering.
A blessed hand like that ought to grip a pen
only when it signs a land contract or a birth certificate;
otherwise, it should be gripping a tennis racket or a lover's hand.
Yet, this hand—its nails, either gray or inky,
with many vertical lines, brittle as oyster shells,
and with no moon peering out of any horizon—
is a hand doomed to keep holding only a pen.
This hand, ashamed of its unhealthiness, must go on
singing only of other hands, beautiful healthy hands.
Yet, if singing, in the end,
only means sensitivity tracing its own sensitivity,
this moment when, as if writing on a mirror, this hand is writing about
itself
is, I must say, wholly poetic and wholly critical.

Myself Departing

A young man, crouched, is tying his shoelaces.
Back turned this way, his nape, how gentle.
The two slowly moving lumps of flesh on the shoulders
and two knees at both sides of his waist are fresh, round
(the male nipples pressed against his knees are still peach-colored).
The reticent young animal's untainted straight gaze
stays on the movements of his fingers tying shoelaces
but the moving fingers themselves are tranced, dreaming
of the time they'll play with the gentle Eros, rolled in thin skin,
dozing in a soft grassbush pregnant with light,
a little above the movements of the fingers tying shoelaces,
below the pliant belly like that of a starved young wolf.
The young man rises and, in his laced boots, naked,
begins to walk, keeps walking, soon grows old.
The man grown old tightens his expression, never turns to look
but behind the man grown old, many times does the young man
        crouch,
tie his shoelaces, rise, and begin to walk
many times.

Myself in the Manner of a Suicide

I will be buried in the road, cut far off from my right hand.
(Because of its behavior the right hand is forever cursed.)
Among the roads, a road with particularly heavy traffic of carts and
　　horses.
Endlessly crisscrossed by the ruts that come and go,
my face will have deep wrinkles imitating agony chiseled into it.
My flesh will rot like a seed potato and, rotting, become transparent;
but because, blocked by the hard surface of the road, it cannot
　　sprout,
in the dark earth my face, my phallus, will meaninglessly multiply.
Rather, from the sinful hand that was cut off and buried
I will bud as a new plant,
but the multiplying me in the earth will never take part in it.
I will become a single tree, spread in the light,
and as a testimony to my self putrefying in the earth, to my self that
　　was once in the sunlight,
will flutter, and blaze, in one spot in the ravaged landscape.
Of that dark blazing face of that dark blazing day,
I now exist as a clumsy copy.

Myself with Cheese

As an embodiment of the word "manducation," for example,
there will be a hunk of cheese with a golden fragrance.
If, to spotlight the manner of its golden embodiment,
the plate on which this hunk of cheese is placed is an ordinary plate of
    tin,
and where the tin plate is is a casual wood table,
what will be the manner of my being with knife in hand, in front of the
    table?
I, as poet, witness this embodiment of gold.
Because it is said that to witness as poet
must be more impersonal than to witness as eater,
before the plate of cheese, my beard is an impersonal beard,
my wet teeth and tongue are impersonal teeth and tongue,
even the lifted knife is an impersonal knife.

Myself at Table

There is a glass. Shallow water at its bottom.
The glass's metal rim is soiled with sauce.
On a large plate, half eaten bread, pork fat, brussels sprouts.
Wet, and scattered about: bits of grape skin and seeds.
Rolled up is a napkin which wiped the mouth that is there.
Probably it is also there that my face and my right hand are.
Things that are soiled, because they are soiled,
let them be blessed.

Myself in the Disguise of a Traveler

Wearing the wide-brimmed hat of one always roaming,
equipped with an ash stick, in a *khlamus*,
I stand barefoot on the road the sun shines on.
The road is precisely the road now before me.
I am forbidden to turn to look,
because, for bad blood, I was driven from my hometown.
The only thing permitted me is the eternally closed villages ahead.
But at the entrance of each village stand many columns crowded with
    birds of sunset,
on each column is a bloody head,
and each bloody head is no other than my head:
because in the village I visit I am a repellent visitor,
who brings the blood smell into its peaceful dailiness.
I, as one without his head, pass through the deserted village,
and having passed, put on my wide-brimmed hat.
Ahead of this village there will be another village of sunset.
At the entrance of the new village there will be more of my heads.
To encounter my own bloody heads, I must keep going.
My blood-reeking walk is what I call the road.

Myself in the Manner of a Troubador

Mounting a horse with an abundant mane and in glittery armor, a
    hero
will have to have a face as dazzling as that orb of day.
But a base one ordered to sing of heroes,
I cannot have a face, however ordinary.

Like a photo of the hateful man an abandoned woman tore into
    shreds,
my face is torn apart and lost in advance.
Faceless, holding in both hands a lyre quite like a face,
on a hill with a view of the field shining with battle dust, under a plane
    tree,

or on a boulder of a cape overlooking the sea where triremes come
    and go,
I sit for thousands of years, I just continue to sit.
The odes that, faceless, I sing in praise of passing heroes
overflow as beautiful blood from the chest wound I hide with the lyre.

Myself in the Image of the King of the Wood

I have no voice. The owl living on a high oak branch has my voice.
I have no shadow. The rustling reeds behind the oak wood have my
   shadow.
I have no gestures. Instead of me, the world beyond the reed lake
has my gestures, swaying.
I have no face. Instead of me, the only person to visit me
will have my unmistakable face.
On a night of a beautiful full moon, from the world beyond the lake,
   he will come.
Rustling the reeds he will cross the lake and dash toward me as I
   stand in the wood to welcome him.
A sword will flash, and voiceless, I will lie fallen by his feet.
That moment I will become him, I will for the first time have a face,
   the face of the one who visits me.
He will become me. He will have become the one to continue to wait
   in the wood,
without a face, without gestures, without a shadow.

Myself as in the Onan Legend

My face will be dark.
The glittering liquid that spurts out of my holy procreative center
will not be received into that contractile interior, which is eternally
     female,
but spill, and keep spilling, on the cold lifeless ground,
so my sons, who are my shadows, will as Little Leeches make a
     round of the earth,
make a round of the water labyrinth at the bottom of the earth, make
     a round of the crisscross paths inside the tree,
and, ejected from the skyward mouth of every leaf at the tip of the
     tree,
will drift aimlessly in the empty blue sky and become lost,
so my face should have been what my sons of the endlessly continu-
     ing
glittering links of light began to weave and ended weaving,
so the overflowing light is behind me, not before me.
My face, the whole face as one large mouth of darkness,
in the overflowing, spilling light, is voicelessly shouting.

Myself in the Disguise of an Ancient Goddess

Young man, you who stand in the stone-paved plaza of this castle
  city,
your history, that you are from the foul countryside,
is revealed in your bare feet not even clad in sandals.
Look, far up the worn stone steps rising from your feet,
look at my frightful face as I stand filling the pantheon.
You who stand precisely at right angles to the ground as an innocent
  sundial
drag not only your own shadow in the summer afternoon,
you are dragging along with you the smell of country soil,
the smells of plants, the smell of water, the smell of cow dung.
I like the ignorant glitter of astonishment in your staring eyes.
I like the youthful darkness, almost fragrant, of your mouth, agape.
My lust must chew up your astonishment, your ignorance, the whole
  of your youth.
My mouth slit to the ears is for kissing you,
for sucking you to the marrow, beginning with the flesh of your lips it
  kisses.
The scarlet of my cheeks must be freshly re-dyed with your blood.
Come, young man, you've stared at me, you no longer can escape
  from me.
Behind the bloody wedding of you and me
the world will burn like the city of sin in the legend.
Our being is always burning like it.

Myself in the Disguise of an Ancient Queen

When did my head become an ancient cow's sacred head?
As that sublime queen of grief with a cow's head,
in search of the torn and lost pieces of flesh of my snake-bodied hus-
    band, the king,
I wander through movie theaters, public bathhouses, street toilets all
    over the world.
Only, the difference between that queen of Egypt and me
is that while the queen gathered up all of her husband's flesh torn into
    fourteen pieces
but could not find one, the phallus,
I gather up innumerable phalluses innumerably, and yet
cannot in the end find one thing, a body.
Every phallus is my husband the king, but also the hateful enemy who
    killed my husband.
I kiss every phallus, throw it away, spit on it, and leave.
The phalluses thrown away drift in foam through the sea called the
    world
and ahead of me, penetrating through movie theaters, public bath-
    houses, street toilets,
various rivers flow, various seas flow,
and the tree of tears sways on the shore of eternity that I cannot reach
    eternally.

The tree of tears hugs a coffin in its hundred octopus tentacles,
a coffin which, blatantly shaped like a phallus,
is the origin of all time and space.

Myself in the Disguise of a Sacred Prostitute

From the face past noon in the handmirror held in my left hand
I meticulously plucked the whiskers one by one.
I shaved my eyebrows, penciled them, pouted my lips and rouged
     them.
I took a wig sprinkled with blue hair powder and put it on, placed a
     goldband on my forehead.
To conceal my larynx, I put on a similar but wider goldband.
I put on bracelets, put on anklets, wear sheepskin sandals,
I put over my head a yellow-worn robe smelly from sweat,
picked teeth, spat out, chewed a fragrant herb.
I rubbed dubious perfumed oil in my armpits and navel
and went out of the mirror, into a gallery of the collapsed pantheon.
Only young gods and travelers passed.
An emerald talking bird perched on an emerald tree and sang:
"You're a man. You're a man. Besides, you are old."
"On the abandoned road where gods and sacred travelers come and
     go,
are not all human beings miserable prostitutes?"
In the emerald evening I wailed aloud.

Myself in the Manner of a Roman Noble

Put me in the palanquin,
carry me to midday throngs,
to the crowds that smell of beasts' cages,
of sweat, of dirt, of puke, of shit

To the din of the day of triumph,
the commotion of the day evil tidings arrive,
the violence of a festival day,
the screams of the day of anger

Crowds to be loved—
ignorant, cruel, lascivious
lumps of flesh that play with one another,
love one another in any place

Pale as the color of the earth,
I'll drown in the sweat of death—
leave me in the palanquin, in the human waves,
then scatter away, get lost

The masses will vie to tear my chest,
pull out my heart, my intestines,
gouge my eyeballs, wrench my cock,
roam with them and lose them

The palanquin, shattered, lies in pieces,
blood dyes the stone pavement.
With the crowd carrying me around
I am everywhere

Myself in the Manner of Christopher

When is it:
on my meager shoulders, the young one I carry increases his weight,
his infantile legs turn into a youth's flesh-packed hirsuite thighs
and squeeze my pointed chin from both sides.

Base lips one straight line, I grit my teeth.
On my forehead where the salt of pain has formed, I make scar-like
wrinkles,
trying to look up at the puzzling infant's transformation, rolling up my
eyes,
under whose black irises, crisscrossing the whites are exhausted jaun-
diced earthworms.

The heavens cleave, a streak of pale viscous light
catches the twitching half of my criminal-like face,
and at the pinnacle of ugly embarrassment, with the youth on my
shoulders I topple.
My knees of skin and bone now squeeze his young neck.

Myself as in *Genesis*

The young man's yard-long hair turns into billowing light and swirls
    up,
the hair that has swirled up parts itself in the middle.
With the hair that has parted into two as wings, beating the air,
naked feet treading the void he comes down to the ground, to this city
    of hell.

Labyrinthine alleys form the city, low eaves line up like a comb's
    teeth.
Men, each coming out of his door of sin, rush in throngs.
Because of their impurities that drip smelly juice from their pores all
    over their bodies,
they must violate the visitor's holy flesh.

Behind the wood door that a thousand hands knock, the visitor's hair
    is already a flame.
The hair that has become a flame burns the door from that side, turns
    it into a board of flames,
and illuminates in precise detail the faces of the men exactly like the
    street map of this hell city.
The faces of the thousand men who resemble one another are, in
    other words, a thousand of me!

Myself in the Manner of
"Telemachus Who Has Returned"

The one who returned was not father,
the one who returned was in fact his son, me.
Did father exist in the first place?
The one who, encased in glittery armor, stood at the castle gate,
was that really father?
The wooden horse for deception, terrible wanderings,
the one-eyed monster, the beautiful evil woman,
weren't all these the fairy tales I wove
from the colored threads of bedtime stories of mother and old folks?
Within the door of the child's room that became an adult's room as it
        was
I went on having the same dream for ten years, for twenty years.
Father? Boat that father was on?
That was me, was my bootless dream bed,
no, it was, you see, a boat I myself went on drifting in.
The one who returned was not father,
the one who returned was in fact his son, me.
No, to tell you the truth, no one returns.
I go on drifting in the ocean the size of my room,
and so, father, even now, goes on drifting
in a world my size.

Myself as in the Narcissus Legend

I pushed two bulbs into the two eye-sockets.
Aching with pounding pain, the bulbs are blind.
Wrapped in skin with bulging light-purple threads,
they are gazing only at the hell inside.

This maddening head is itself a bulb.
The heavy bulb above the neck, drawn by the bulbs in the crotch,
tilts toward the center of the mirror labyrinth, the dark water,
the deep water bottom, the dizzying water gimlet.

Myself . . . If I Were a Leper

If, covered with a holy white robe,
I were a leper,
would you open the door for me
when I stand at your gate in the morning?

Would you accept
without edging back
the coal-black imploration of my coal-black eyes,
the only part showing from the white robe?

Would you drop a coin of pity
on the hole-ridden palm that I hold out?
Inside the white robe, my face and my heart
are molten, like a forge.

Myself in an Anatomical Chart
of Sexual Intercourse

The tip of my existence, the soldering iron of wet, hot flesh,
inserted in a death smith's gentle forge, quickly increases its volume.
The iron turns red hot, the iron turns white hot, and at the pinnacle of
    white heat, finally, melts from its cusp.
O, spurting, white-muddied, thick liquid at the moment of existence
    metastasizing into nothingness!
The liquid spreads like a cloud and enters the womb, depths of the
    burning forge.
But look, the one who has accepted my existence, is not facing me.
The tongue tip sharpened like a hook swims in the air, trembling.
So, what I am invading is no womb, but a flexible male rectum.
From rectum to oral cavity, what puzzling swells and coils of entrails!
Like Arabian labyrinths, like the ant holes the legendary bull inhabits,
like a thunderhead's interlacing corridors, they are entangled, com-
    plicated.
My liquid, which is myself, invading every labyrinth,
every ant hole, and every corridor, all at once spreads throughout
    him.
But look again, this invader is not me,
rather, the one invaded is no one but me!
I have, by a true existence, my rectum bloodied and disgraced,
and from my tip twitching in painful bliss, into space,
not the thick liquid, but feeble air is radiated,
and continues to be radiated.

Myself with a Motorcycle

Motorcycle, the vehicle for long-haired young gods.
My god sports a glans-shaped jeweled crown we call a helmet,
sticks his legs with long shins into azure jeans
puts on heavy boots adorned with many golden studs,
and dashes through the twilight of purple gods.
At the moment, midway on the stone steps behind a theater, for ex-
    ample,
my god is in the midst of a blood-reeking conspiratorial discussion
    with other long-haired gods.
Their youthful conspiracy is too dazzling, too fragrant
for me, passing the foot of the stone steps, to clearly discern.
Below the stairs, only the god's seat made of steel gleams like a living
    thing.
I touch the motorcycle, particularly that part of its seat which was just
    glued to the ass of my god,
still retaining the ass's warmth.
My god eats Kentucky fried chicken, drinks Coca-Cola,
and from the dawn-colored slit of his beautiful ass he ejects shit.

Myself with a Glory Hole

Lord, when will it be?
Will it be long before Your visit?
I crouch on the opprobrious floor, waiting, while before me
are pictures of angels with wings, and of saints;
at the center of the wall adorned with holy words of gold and silver,
a holy hole—Your shining visitation through it,
is it not yet time for it?
O then, I would kneel before You,
madly open my lips parched and cracked from thirst,
and as that terrifying prophet said,
fill my mouth with You.
Inside my mouth You would quickly grow large,
Your holy basket would violently overflow and splatter,
and to my popping eyes, my short nose,
to my crewcut head with a lot of young gray hair,
and to my narrow forehead, splatter all over, drip lazily,
and like trails of slugs, glutinously gleam—
in Your incomparable compassion, like one raped
I would close my eyes as if suffering, and pant. . . .
When will that be? Will it be long before the visit?

These words said, the face, like a pig-skin sack from which liquor has
    leaked,
deflated into wrinkles, was folded on its neck,
and together with the body mounting the john, slumped.
The perplexing incident just over, before the john
stood the wall filled with base graffiti,
and from the other side of the hole in the middle of the wall, a glaring
parched eye was looking in.

Myself in Fake Doric Style

What's here is neither a grassfield a breeze goes across nor a
   haystack fragrant of sun
but a bland standardized iron bed seen in a hospital or dormitory,
though, to make up for it, through an ordinary, rose-patterned, fake
   lace curtain
the sun shines in, late morning pastoral, truly pastoral sunlight.

The pastoral smell, from the other side of the door—when we finally
   get into bed,
on the other side of the iron door, is the smell of pasteurized country
   the milkman left in the milkbox.
We uncover from the blanket our naked back down to the point
   below Michael's lozenge,
hold a cigarette roll cut at both ends in our mouth gone sticky with
   deathsmell, and light it.

Peaceful fire burns noisily up the roll, *Peace* fire,
from the depths of the radio, Paul McCartney
cloying, wearily whisperes O a fake pastorale, a fake love song.
The song's singing of roses, yesterday's roses, which bloom on
   hedges.

On our back as well, dots of roses, blood-colored roses,
roses of claws and teeth which love bored stiff, or rather jealousy out
   of habit, has made to bloom,
not so much roses as stains of dead leaves will someday cover the
   two backs
of us—that is, me the one who loves, and me again, the one who is
   loved.

Myself through the Image of a Mirror

Break the mirror, every mirror there is, all the mirrors called mirrors,
because the road before me, the boy who comes this way on the
    road,
the foliage that glistens in the afternoon sun, the purling beyond the
    foliage,
the sky full of gentle blue, the shape of a bird sucked into layers of
    blue,
the world that waylays us with transparent glamors, are every one of
    them a mirror,
because the word, world, the word, blue, the words, purling, foliage,
    boy,
the word is another mirror which, face to face with the world, lies in
    wait,
because everything that is reflected in the mirror is myself, therefore
    the world is myself, therefore the word is myself,
and the same myself is merely made up of innumerable fragments of a
    mirror.
Break the mirror, smash the mirror, don't put a new mirror beyond
    the shattered mirror.
In any labyrinth behind the broken, smashed, shattered mirror,
I'm not found, I'm not found, not found!

Myself by the Last Fire

Not the flames climbing a tower of firewood stacked in parallel
    crosses
but burners' businesslike fire will burn me.
I will shed tears, crackle all over my body,
but will not rise to my feet like an ancient king.
That won't be appropriate for burners' prosaic fire.
Nonetheless, myself one hundred years old . . . myself fifty years old
    . . . myself thirty-seven years old,
myself ten years old . . . and one year old will crackle all at once,
all of my selves that crackle will shed tears at once,
split, and split into minuscule fragments of the world.
The billions of split fragments will separately own my billions of
    selves.
If, once, unknown mysterious fire synthesized my billions of selves,
kneaded them, and made them into my one self,
burners' prosaic fire that burns me will also be mysterious fire.
At the time of that mysterious fire by which my one self was made
I likewise must have been shedding beautiful tears.

from
A BUNCH OF KEYS
(published 1982)

This Morning, Her Majesty the Queen

This morning, Her Majesty the Queen, whose benevolence and compassion are unequaled, had the heads of seven rebels sawed off with deliberate slowness in the yard facing the Breakfast Room, instead of listening to the matutinal debate on the affairs of state. The seven rebels, ranging from sixteen to twenty-one in age, were all from a proud tribe inhabiting the mountainous region near the border. When the last one condemned to death spewed at Her Majesty dreadfully base words along with opprobrious spit, she raised her finger to order that her breakfast on the table be taken away.

This morning, Her Majesty the Queen, who is incomparable in making light of herself, had no particular appetite. All she had for breakfast was black goat's milk, a dormouse cooked with truffles, a pot-broiled honeybird, fried papaya slices, cheese of mule's milk, and sugar-pickled quinces, three of which she ate. She left tooth-marks on a fourth but went no further. As usual, the eighty-year-old eunuch and the eight-year-old eunuch helped her rinse her fingers, using the pitcher and bowl made of seven kinds of jewels.

This morning, Her Majesty the Queen, whose modesty is known to the four directions, sat astride the toilet for half an hour. Today's toilet was made of gold and was boat-shaped, its lower half of wave patterns inlaid with jaspers each the size of a pine cone. That part of the toilet that Her Majesty's buttocks came in contact with was covered by layers of soft cloth woven by transparent moths of a distant country, which is as valuable as gold. Although Her Majesty, who normally tends to be costive, strained so hard that sweat poured like cataracts over her forehead and back, she only broke wind several times, sounding like a squashed frog, and let out two pieces of feces like rabbit droppings. After the toilet, a blind armless slave washed and wiped her buttocks and vagina with the perfume-soaked tip of his tongue.

This morning, Her Majesty the Queen, who is stern in controlling herself, cast off her rainbow-hued robes one by one, entered the Bathing Room, and played with seven virgin girls who still do not know men. Her magnanimity is boundless: she treated each virgin like her own sister and went so far as to press the virgin's breasts with her palms while letting her gracious lips and tongue crawl over the virgin's inner thighs. She was extremely displeased with a particularly beautiful one who was too conscious of her station, and gave her the punishment of one thousand lashes. If the virgin fortunately breathes her last at the end of the whipping, a large number of gold coins will be given to her parents.

This morning, Her Majesty the Queen, whose thought never leaves the glory of her State and her people, entered the Dressing Room at the top of the palace that has only four columns standing and no walls or windows; she then had the gray hair of her private parts pulled, had her eyelids lifted, had the nails of her fingers and toes painted scarlet, and had a perfumed oil rubbed into her armpits, thighs, and nipples with special meticulousness. To obtain a single jar of this perfumed oil, extremely dangerous seafaring expeditions are annually set up, and most of the national treasury and the lives of hundreds and thousands of young soldiers are expended. But its fragrance is truly aromatic and, mingling with the scent from her armpits and loins, reaches the noses of the porters in the disorderly marketplace way below, who do not know what to do with their excess energy.

This morning, Her Majesty the Queen, whose devoutness does not even have to be mentioned, climbed, after putting herself in the proper costume, to the Shrine of Ten Thousand Deities at the innermost part, at the highest point of the palace. Her Majesty, recognizing that the smoke going out of the hole open to heaven in the great dome was visibly feeble, permitted the current number of sacrificial people to be doubled. To the chief priest who stared at her with some unease, she declared with admirable casualness that the only thing to be done was to double the current war efforts.

This morning, Her Majesty the Queen, who is almost savage in suppressing her personal emotions, asked a passing administrator about the Prince, from the palanquin that was taking her through a corridor from one political duty to another. The Prince, though her true son, became uneasy about the excessive delay of the ceremony of installing him as Crown Prince and committed the imprudence of initiating a rebellion against his own mother, Her Majesty. At one time half of the population sided with him, and Her Majesty was even imprisoned. By her wise ploy of exposing her breasts and appealing to his affections as a blood relation, the situation was reversed. Those aides who took the Prince's side were mercilessly killed, and the Prince has since been incarcerated in the depths of the conspiratorially complex labyrinth in the base of the palace. Learning that the Prince is given meatballs with minuscule doses of deadly poison every day, and that his insanity has rapidly worsened in recent days, Her Majesty did not even twitch her face.

This morning, Her Majesty the Queen, whose wisdom is obvious to everyone, put the ceremonial beard to her chin, wore the ceremonial great sword, and met three emissaries of a friendly nation and a young nobleman from a tributary nation. All her words were spoken on her behalf by her minister, and each time he finished speaking, she thoughtfully nodded and shook the bell at the end of the grip of her sword. Only, she was gracious enough to give special words to the young nobleman of the tributary nation, who was supple as a young buck, and invited him to share lunch with her in her Bedroom. As a gesture of acceptance, the nobleman, needless to say, kneeled before Her Majesty and kissed the toes of her elephantine legs.

This morning, Her Majesty the Queen, who is too busy tending to affairs of state . . . but in the courtyard where white peacocks with clipped wings play, the sundial already points to noon. In Her Majesty's Bedroom, the table speckled with mother-of-pearl and as large as her bed is loaded with dishes and bowls of rare foods and awaits the entrance of Her Majesty and her young guest. Her Majesty ordered that before the meal, two large cups of mead mixed with panther's milk and barberry root be readied.

We Do Not Know the Name of the King

The king is someone who came from the dark water at the end of the
   east
Still, we do not know his true name
The king is a fist raised toward the shadow land at the end of the west
Still, we do not know his true name
The king is ten toes and two heels that crush and grind the people
Still, we do not know his true name
The king is a dazzling head which, lost in clouds, is invisible
Still, we do not know his true name
The king is the command is to do this and that that drop from a dizzy-
   ing height
Still, we do not know his true name
The king is a heart that pulses eternally with timeless earth
Still, we do not know his true name
The king is the lusts that spurt up unstoppably toward the sun
Still, we do not know his true name

We send, for the king, ships of trade toward a thousand unknown
   ports
Still, we do not know his true name
We offer, for the king, the blood of one thousand people in a field at
   the border
Still, we do not know his true name
We continue, for the king, to plow, our legs enfeebled in the mud
Still, we do not know his true name
We dig, for the king, coarse metals in the depths of the ground, blind
Still, we do not know his true name
We willingly leave, for the king, the women of our households to
   humiliation
Still, we do not know his true name
We are, for the king, robbed of the last bit of grain in our coffer
Still, we do not know his true name
We build, for the king, an everlasting abode, shortening our lives
Still, we do not know his true name

106

The king, some say, was once a base slave at the end of the east
The king's fist raised toward the end of the west, some say, is infested
with leprosy
The king, some say, is fearful of his closest aides and defecates on
the stool brought in under his bed
The king, some say, is a shabby-looking old man less than five feet
tall
The king's voice giving commands, some say, is as irritable and high-
pitched as that of a hysterical woman
The king's heart, some say, is constantly watched by ten doctors for
its irregular pulse
The king's phallus, some say, always droops like the clothbelt of his
robe
Of the king's one thousand ships, some say, nine hundred ninety-nine
never return
The one thousand people for the king's blood offering, some say, are
collected from his own land
The king's mud, some say, is packed full of worms that destroy this
land
The king's diggers of coarse metals, some say, have revolted at the
end of the south
The women taken away for the king, some say, merely tire him
The king's key to his granary is in the minister's pouch, some say, and
the king is starved
The king's everlasting abode, some say, is plundered to the last bit,
though far from completed

Still, we do not know the king's true name

Mutsuo Takahashi

1937   Born December 15 to a steelworker in the steel city Yahata, Kyushu.

1938   His father dies. Thereafter, separated from his mother, lives with a variety of relatives and other families.

1944   Enters elementary school. Begins to live in the port town Moji with his mother, who had returned from China in the previous year.

1945   End of the war. Begins to write poems.

1959   Publishes his first book of poems, Mino, My Bull* (Mino, Watashi no Oushi). Has TB and spends a year and nine months in a sanatorium. During this time, becomes acquainted with Friar Tsuda and takes an interest in Catholicism. Reads the Bible and Greek tragedies.

1962   Graduates from Fukuoka University of Education and moves to Tokyo.

1964   Publishes Rose Tree, Fake Lovers* (Bara no Ki, Nise no Koibito-tachi). Becomes acquainted with Yukio Mishima.

1965   Publishes Sleeping, Sinning, Falling+ (Nemuri to Okashi to Rakka to).

1966   Publishes You Dirty Ones, Do Dirtier Things*+ (Yogoretaru Mono wa Sara no Yogoretaru Koto o Nase).

1969   Begins work on Twelves Perspective (Juni no Enkei), an autobiographical novel. Travels to Israel, Turkey, Greece, Italy, and France.

1970   Publishes Twelve Perspectives. Mishima commits suicide.

1971   Lives in New York City for forty days in April and May. In August, travels to Belgium, Italy, France, and England. Publishes Ode*+ (Homeuta).

1972   Publishes a collection of novellas, Holy Triangle (Sei Sankakkei), and a book of poems, King of the Calendar (Koyomi no O).

1973   Travels to Mexico. Publishes a book of haiku.

1974   Travels to Korea. Publishes a novel, Zen's Pilgrimage (Zen no Henreki), and a book of poems, Verbs I (Doshi I).

1975   Travels to England, Spain, Morocco, Portugal, and Taiwan. Friar Tsuda dies. Publishes Self-portraits 50+ (Watakushi). [Poems of a Penisist, a selection of his poems in English translation, published in the United States.]

1976   From the end of the previous year to January this year, travels to Egypt. Publishes a collection of essays. With two other poets, starts a magazine, Symposium (Kyoen).

1977   Travels to Israel and Greece. Publishes two collections of essays and a book of haiku.

1978   Helps revise a translation of Euripides' *Medea* for production at Nissei Theater. Publishes two collections of essays and a book of tanka.

1979   Helps revise a translation of *Notre-Dame de Paris* for production at Nissei Theater. Travels to New York in July and to San Francisco in September. Publishes a collection of essays and a book of poems, *At A Place Called Wandering + (Sasurai to iu Na no Chi nite)*.

1980   Travels to Germany, Austria, Hong Kong, and Algeria.

1981   Experiences difficulty in writing poems.

1982   Travels to Hong Kong. On May 7, injured in a traffic accident. Publishes two books of poems, *The Structure of the Kingdom (Okoku no Kozo)* and *A Bunch of Keys + (Kagitaba)*. Receives the 20th Rekitei Prize for *The Structure of the Kingdom*.

* Partially or wholly translated in *Poems of a Penisist* (Chicago Review Press, 1975).

+ Partially or wholly translated in this book.

OTHER TITLES IN THE CROSSING PRESS GAY SERIES:

THE CONNECTICUT COUNTESS, Gay Chronicles of Davey Bryant
by David Watmough. Story-telling at its best, told with zest. The
lively life of Davey from adolescence to middle-age. $6.95 paper

ON THE LINE, New Gay Fiction edited by Ian Young. Eighteen stories
by writers such as Edmund White, Wm. Burroughs, Felice Picano,
James Purdy, etc. $6.95 paper

THE GAY TOUCH, Stories by Peter Robins. Eleven amusing stories
with the gay touch by an English writer. "Pure irony, refreshingly
unmoralized" (Times Literary Supplement). $4.95 paper

SON OF THE MALE MUSE, A Gay Poetry Anthology edited by Ian
Young. Nearly three dozen poets of the 80s—a frank and lyrical look
at gay sensibility today. Photographs of contributors. $7.95 paper

THE MALE MUSE, Gay Poetry Anthology edited by Ian Young. The
first of its kind with all the great poets including Allen Ginsberg, Paul
Goodman, Christopher Isherwood, Robert Duncan, Tennessee
Williams. $5.95 paper

THE TENDERNESS OF THE WOLVES by Dennis Cooper with Intro.
by Edmund White. A powerful collection of gay-punk poems by a
poet who doesn't flinch. $4.95 paper.

FROM THE DIARY OF PETER DOYLE And Other Poems by John
Gill. Narrative poem about Walt Whitman's companion, Peter Doyle
plus other lyrics—passionate and moving. $4.50 paper.

You can get these books from your local bookstore or directly from
The Crossing Press, Box 640, Trumansburg, N.Y. 14886. When order-
ing from us please send check or money order and add $1.00 postage
and handling charge.